INSIDE THE
STEEL INDUSTRY

by Carla Mooney

Content Consultant

Emmanuel De Moor

Assistant Professor
George S. Ansell Department of Metallurgical and
Materials Engineering
Colorado School of Mines

BIG
BUSINESS

Essential Library

An Imprint of Abdo Publishing | abdopublishing.com

abdopublishing.com

Published by Abdo Publishing, a division of ABDO, PO Box 398166, Minneapolis, Minnesota 55439. Copyright © 2017 by Abdo Consulting Group, Inc. International copyrights reserved in all countries. No part of this book may be reproduced in any form without written permission from the publisher. Essential Library™ is a trademark and logo of Abdo Publishing.

Printed in the United States of America, North Mankato, Minnesota
102016
012017

THIS BOOK CONTAINS
RECYCLED MATERIALS

Cover Photo: Shutterstock Images
Interior Photos: Anna Omelchenko/Shutterstock Images, 4; Mark Sykes/Science Source, 6; Alexander Tolstykh/Shutterstock Images, 8; Shutterstock Images, 11, 36, 74–75; Huguette Roe/Shutterstock Images, 13 (top left); M. Khebra/Shutterstock Images, 13 (top right); XXLPhoto/Shutterstock Images, 13 (bottom left); Zhao Jian Kang/Shutterstock Images, 13 (bottom right); Science Source, 14; E. R. Degginger/Science Source, 16; Sheila Terry/Science Source, 19; DeAgostini/Getty Images, 23; SPL/Science Source, 24; Hulton Archive/Getty Images, 29, 52; Bettmann/Getty Images, 31, 44; David E. Scherman/The LIFE Picture Collection/Getty Images, 33; Universal History Archive/UIG/Getty Images, 34; SSPL/Getty Images, 40; Photo Researchers/Science Source, 42; Everett Historical/Shutterstock Images, 50; Oesterreichsches Volkshochschularchiv/Imagno/Getty Images, 54; Wade H. Massie/Shutterstock Images, 57; Alfred Eisenstaedt/The LIFE Picture Collection/Getty Images, 60–61; AP Images, 62, 70, 72; Reinhard Tiburzy/Shutterstock Images, 76–77; Red Line Editorial, 79, 96–97; Jiji Press/AFP/Getty Images, 84; Pan Demin/Shutterstock Images, 86; Svilen Georgiev/Shutterstock Images, 89; Ulrich Baumgarten/Getty Images, 91; Melanie Stetson Freeman/The Christian Science Monitor/AP Images, 93

Editor: Arnold Ringstad
Series Designer: Craig Hinton

Publisher's Cataloging-in-Publication Data

Names: Mooney, Carla, author.
Title: Inside the steel industry / by Carla Mooney.
Description: Minneapolis, MN : Abdo Publishing, 2017. | Series: Big business |
    Includes bibliographical references and index.
Identifiers: LCCN 2016945209 | ISBN 9781680783735 (lib. bdg.) |
    ISBN 9781680797268 (ebook)
Subjects: LCSH: Steel industry and trade --Juvenile literature. | Steel products--
    Juvenile literature.
Classification: DDC 338.4--dc23
LC record available at http://lccn.loc.gov/2016945209

Contents

1 STEEL: A CRITICAL INDUSTRY

For more than a century, steel has been an integral part of daily life. People prepare meals in stainless steel cookware and ride steel train cars on steel rails to work in steel-framed skyscrapers. Orthodontists straighten teeth with steel braces, while surgeons operate with steel scalpels. As the uses for steel have expanded over the past 50 years, its weaknesses have mostly remained the same. Like other metals, steel is vulnerable to the corrosive effects of water and salt and the abrasive effects of materials such as sand. But in 2015, researchers at Harvard University announced they had found a way to improve this crucial metal.

The researchers created a new surface coating for steel. They announced the coating could repel any type of liquid, making the steel stronger and more durable. "This research is an example of hard core, classic material science," said Harvard's Joanna Aizenberg. "We took a material that changed the world and asked, how can we make it better?"[1]

From cars on the streets to enormous skyscrapers, modern cities are built largely from steel.

Adding new coatings can help change the properties of steel.

The biggest challenge for researchers in developing the surface coating was figuring out a way to protect the steel without affecting its performance. The researchers used an electrochemical technique to place an extremely thin film of small and rough patches of tungsten oxide, known as islands, directly onto a steel surface. Tungsten oxide is a chemical compound that contains oxygen and the element tungsten, which is very hard. If one part of the tungsten film is destroyed or damaged, the remaining tungsten oxide islands still protect the steel because the islands are not connected.

The Harvard researchers tested the surface coating by scratching it with a variety of tools, including stainless steel tweezers and instruments with diamond tips. They hit it with thousands of hard, heavy beads. They also tested the surface coating's ability to repel a variety of liquids, including water, oil, fluids containing bacteria and blood, and highly corrosive liquids. The coating repelled all of the liquids and resisted bacterial contamination. In addition, the researchers discovered during their testing that steel coated with tungsten oxide was stronger than steel without the coating. The Harvard surface coating could be used to improve many steel products. Using it to coat steel medical tools, such as implants and scalpels, is one of the most promising future applications.

The surface coating may one day be used to improve 3-D printing. Layer by layer, 3-D printers build three-dimensional objects. Like all steel objects, the steel components of 3-D printers can become corroded. When printing with thick and sticky materials, the steel nozzles often clog. Covering the nozzles with the new coating could help them deliver the material smoothly and evenly. With less clogging, the lifespan of the printer's steel nozzles would improve.

The US Navy may also benefit from the steel coating. Every year, the navy spends millions of dollars cleaning the hulls of its ships. Barnacles and algae cling to steel hulls. These organisms create drag in the water, which decreases the ship's performance and increases the amount of fuel it uses. Current antifouling paints contain ingredients that are harmful to the environment. An improved steel coating could be a cleaner, cheaper alternative.

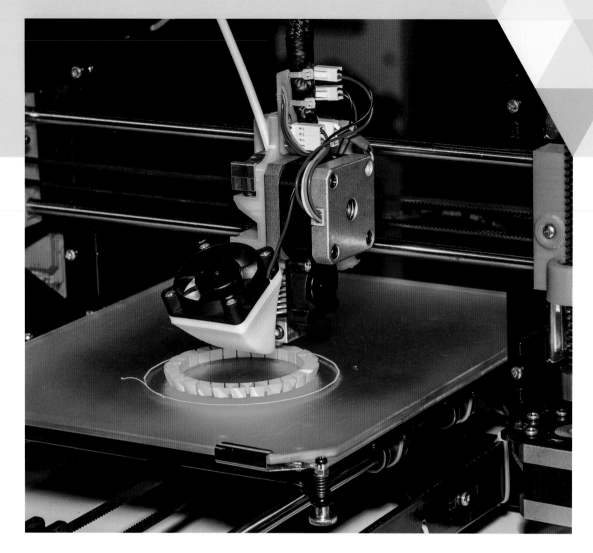

Cutting-edge 3-D printers are among the many products that could see benefits from new steel technologies.

STEEL: THE BACKBONE OF MANUFACTURING

Steel is an alloy in which iron is mixed with carbon. Steel can contain other metals, such as manganese, nickel, or chromium. Different types of steel have different properties. Changing the amount of carbon in steel can change these properties. For example, the steel in a pair of scissors is harder than the steel in a can of fruit. This occurs because the steel in the scissors contains much more carbon than the can, increasing its hardness.

Innovations such as the tungsten oxide coating are making steel more useful than ever. The steel industry continues to be a cornerstone of American business. A unique and vital material, steel is an integral part of a huge variety of products and structures. It is no exaggeration to say the steel industry has helped to build the modern United States. Steel provides the structure and support for famous landmarks such as the Golden Gate Bridge in San Francisco, California; the Gateway Arch in Saint Louis, Missouri; and the One World Trade Center skyscraper in New York City.

Carbon Steel

The majority of steel produced is carbon steel, which contains a small amount of carbon. Steels with between 0.05 and 0.25 percent carbon are low-carbon steels. They are relatively soft and easy to shape. Steels with up to 1 percent carbon are called high-carbon steels.[2] High-carbon steels are usually hard and brittle. A variety of products are made from carbon steels, such as car bodies, steel cans, and engine parts.

In addition to building these landmarks, steel touches almost every part of modern life. People around the world rely on steel for housing, transportation, energy production, tools, health care, and food and water supplies. "We enjoy the benefits of steel in all aspects of our lives. From the moment we wake up until we go to sleep at night, we rely on steel in almost every aspect of our day," says Thomas Gibson, president and CEO of the American Iron and Steel Institute. He continues:

Types of Steels

Alloy steels contain elements such as chromium, copper, manganese, nickel, or silicon, in addition to iron and carbon. These elements give alloy steels additional properties as compared to carbon steels. They are often stronger and harder than carbon steels.

Tool steels are made with added elements such as nickel and tungsten to make them especially strong. These steels are used to make tools and machine parts. Tool steels are usually tempered to make them tough. In tempering, steel is heated to a high temperature and then cooled very quickly. Then it is heated again at a lower temperature.

Many household items are made with stainless steels. This type of steel contains high amounts of chromium and nickel. Stainless steels resist corrosion. They are easy to clean, polish, and sterilize.

In the kitchen, our refrigerator is made of steel—and so many other appliances have steel components. On our way to the office, a job site or to school, we rely on the safety of steel to reinforce our roads, define our bridges and form the body of our cars and trucks. As we glance out our windows we may notice that signs, guardrails, railroad tracks, construction cranes, pipes, commercial buildings and telephone utility poles are all made of steel. And even though we may not notice, the computers we use 24-7 have steel in them.[3]

BUILDING A SUSTAINABLE FUTURE

Steel also has an important role in the world's sustainable future. One of the biggest challenges facing countries worldwide is the growing need for sustainable energy. As energy demands increase and fossil fuel reserves are depleted, steel will be an integral part of delivering renewable energy.

The structural strength of steel enables the building of tall wind turbine towers that can catch high winds hundreds of feet above the ground.

Modern steel can build taller, stronger, and lighter-weight towers for wind turbines. Roofing systems using solar power combine photovoltaic cells with steel panels coated in zinc. In the fields of wind, solar, wave, and tidal power, steel is an essential element for renewable energy.

Steel is also an important part of a variety of sustainable products. High-strength steels are strong and light, allowing less steel to deliver the same amount of strength. Using these steels, manufacturers can create lighter vehicles which require less fuel and release less emissions. Such steels are also used to build energy-efficient appliances. They frame energy efficient buildings, too.

Steel Automobiles

According to the International Organization of Motor Vehicle Manufacturers, 90.1 million vehicles were produced worldwide in 2015, a 1.1 percent increase compared to 2014. Approximately 12 million of them were built in the United States.[7] On average, approximately 2,000 pounds (900 kg) of steel is used in each vehicle.[8] Nearly every new vehicle uses high-strength steels, which makes them lighter, safer, and more fuel efficient. The steel strengthens the body structure, panels, and doors, and it provides energy absorption to protect passengers during a crash. Inside the vehicle, the drivetrain uses steel to create wear-resistant gears. More steel is found in the wheels, tires, and fuel tank, as well as in the steering and braking systems.

Once made, steel can be used again and again. In fact, steel is the world's most recycled material. More steel is recycled each year than aluminum, copper, paper, glass, and plastic combined. According to the World Steel Association, more than 65 million short tons (59 million metric tons) of steel are recycled each year.[4] This number is expected to grow as more communities develop local recycling programs. Steel is also continuously recyclable, which means it can be recycled many times without affecting its performance. In addition, more than 97 percent of by-products from steel manufacturing can be reused.[5] For example, the slag formed in steel production can be used to make concrete. "Steel plays a key role in the new circular business model in which all products must be designed and manufactured to be repaired, remanufactured, reused and recycled," says Edwin Basson, the Director General of the World Steel Association.

"Steel, thanks to its strength, adaptability, flexibility and durability, is the essential material in the circular economy."[6]

Steel Recycling

In the modern steel industry, steel is constantly cycling through a recycling process. Recycled steel, along with iron ore and other raw materials, is processed and used to create new steel products. When those products wear out or are disposed of, they become scrap steel and eventually are processed into yet more products.

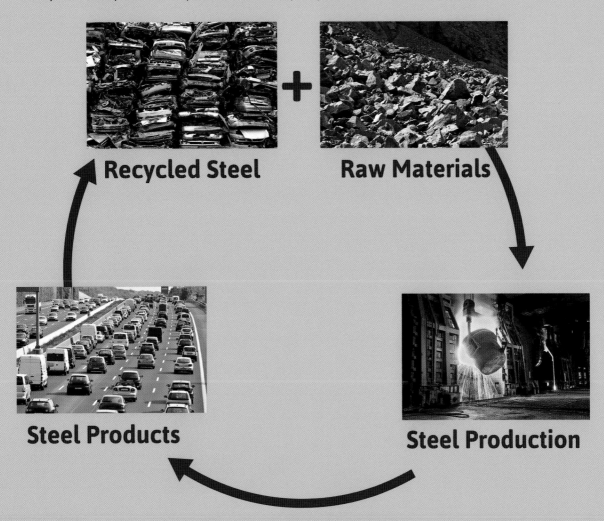

Recycled Steel **Raw Materials**

Steel Products **Steel Production**

2 | EARLY DAYS OF STEEL

Steel is synonymous with many aspects of the modern world, but its origins go back thousands of years. Ancient people discovered nuggets of gold, silver, and copper alongside ordinary rocks. When they tried to chip the nuggets as they did stones, they discovered the metals were malleable and could be hammered or pressed into shapes without breaking or cracking. With this knowledge, they learned how to beat the metals to create simple tools such as knives and sickles. They found the metal tools lasted longer than traditional stone ones. They also hammered the metals into ornaments, jewelry, and other decorative objects for trade.

SMELTING ORE

Beginning around 4000 BCE, ancient people made another important discovery. If they heated certain dull rocks in a fire and waited, shiny lumps of gold, silver, and copper appeared in the fire's ashes. The rocks were ores, types of rock that contain elements that can be extracted. When an ore is heated beyond its melting point in a process called smelting, the metal elements separate from the rock. After discovering smelting, people were no longer limited by how many nuggets of raw

People figured out many of the basic principles of working with ores and metals thousands of years ago.

Chalcopyrite, the most common copper ore, contains copper, iron, and sulfur. metal they could find. Now, they could use ore to produce much more of these valuable materials.

Metalworkers gathered ores and dumped them into fires. They collected the lumps of metal left in the ash. Copper was particularly attractive. At the time, most weapons and tools were made from bone, stone, clay, or tough reeds and wood. Easy to separate from its ore, smelted copper was superior in many ways to these materials. Unlike bone or stone, copper could be hammered into shape. And unlike clay, it could bend and regain its shape. Tougher than reeds or saplings, it could not be sawed through. Metalworkers could even pour melted copper into molds. When they wanted to change the copper's shape, they could melt and reshape it. Around 3000 BCE, metalworkers made another discovery. They discovered if they mixed two or more metals together, they could make an alloy, a metal that was even stronger and more resistant to corrosion. When they mixed molten tin into the copper, they created a metal alloy called bronze. It was used to make tools, weapons, and other objects.

IRON: METAL FROM THE SKY

Another metal was valued even more than copper and bronze. As early as 4000 BCE, ancient people used iron from meteorites to make tools, weapons, and other objects. The word *iron* comes from an ancient word meaning "metal from the sky."[1] Iron was even tougher and stronger than bronze. Yet for centuries, metalworkers were unable to smelt iron from rock and could only use the bits they found in meteorites. When they tried to separate the iron metal from iron ore, the smelting process produced spongy lumps of iron mixed with sludgy impurities. Around 1800 BCE, people discovered that if they smelted the iron ore, hammered the spongy material, reheated it, and hammered it again several times, they could produce an iron metal that was stronger than bronze.

Around 1500 BCE, the Hittite people living in Anatolia, part of modern-day Turkey, began smelting iron on a regular basis. Some of the first iron furnaces were simple rounded hearths in which they used charcoal, a substance produced from heated wood, to heat the iron ore to very high temperatures. The heating process caused a hot, spongy, porous mass of mostly pure iron to form, mixed with slag, bits of charcoal, and other impurities from the ore. A blacksmith would remove the spongy material from the fire and hammer it to force out the charcoal cinders and slag. Hammering also compacted the iron particles. The result was a new type of iron—wrought iron. It contained a trace amount of carbon from the charcoal fire, which made the metal tough and malleable. Through most of the Iron Age, which began around 1200 BCE and lasted until approximately 550 BCE, wrought iron was the most commonly produced metal.

What Is Iron?

Iron is a chemical element on the periodic table. Its symbol is *Fe*. It is a strong, hard, magnetic, silvery-gray metal. Iron is one of the most common elements on Earth and makes up approximately 5 percent of the planet's crust. Earth's core is made almost entirely of iron. Iron can be found naturally in iron ore. In addition to iron, the ore contains various amounts of other elements, including silicon, sulfur, manganese, and phosphorus.

The Iron Age brought more sophisticated technology than had been used in the Bronze Age.

Early ironworkers had one complaint about wrought iron. It could not be melted and poured into molds like other metals such as gold, silver, copper, and bronze. Sometimes, liquid iron leaked out of the bottom of their furnaces. But when it hardened, they could not work it. It was brittle and cracked when hammered. Even when heated like wrought iron, it broke under a hammer's blow.

Over time, some improvements were made to the process of smelting iron. Ironworkers added a goatskin bellows to fan the fire. The bellows forced air into the furnace. It was stronger and more easily controlled than natural drafts of air. More durable furnaces could be reused over and over. Ironworkers layered charcoal and iron ore into an opening in the furnace's front and closed it with clay. After smelting, they broke through the opening again to remove the melted iron. Some ironworkers built better furnaces, which allowed them to put the charcoal and iron ore into the top of the furnace, while the melted iron could be removed from the bottom.

Cast Iron

When heated at very high temperatures, iron begins to absorb carbon rapidly. Absorbing the carbon lowers the iron's melting point, and the iron begins to melt. It becomes cast iron, which contains approximately 3 to 4.5 percent carbon.[2] Unlike wrought iron, melted cast iron can be poured into molds to form specific shapes. The high percentage of carbon, however, also makes cast iron hard and brittle. It is more likely to crack or shatter with a heavy blow. It cannot be heated and hammered into shape, a process called forging. Eventually, iron makers learned how to turn cast iron into more useful wrought iron by removing the excess carbon.

Over several centuries, knowledge of iron making spread from community to community across Europe and Asia. People used iron to make pots, tools, axes, and blades. Iron made life easier. It replaced bronze and stone tools. With iron farming tools such as sickles and plough tips, farmers were able to work tough soils, plant new crops, and work faster. With efficient iron tools, families had more time to spend on other activities such as jewelry-making, sewing clothes, or producing salt for trade.

STEEL: AN ACCIDENTAL DISCOVERY

There is no specific record of the discovery of steel. It most likely happened by accident. When early ironworkers heated iron ore in charcoal fires, it produced a spongy mass of iron. This mass could be hammered or wrought into a shape. But if the iron was left in the fire for a longer period of time, it grew harder and stronger. And if the material was repeatedly heated, folded, and hammered, it became even stronger. Today, steelmakers know steel is a combination of iron, a small amount of carbon, and other trace elements. By heating the iron ore in a charcoal fire, which contained carbon, some carbon transferred to the iron to create steel. Early iron makers did not understand the chemistry of steel. Even so, they recognized its value.

The new steel could be worked like iron, but it was stronger and could make a sharper edge. Iron Age craftsmen worked with steel to create tools and weapons. They developed new techniques such as quench hardening, the rapid cooling of hammered steel in water or oil to increase its hardness. Still, steelmaking was a long and difficult process. The quality of the sword or tool depended on the

Blast Furnaces and Pig Iron

In the late Middle Ages, European makers of cast iron developed the blast furnace, which was a tall chimneylike structure. Each furnace was approximately 10 feet (3 m) high and shaped like an hourglass. Workers fitted bellows at the bottom to pump in air. Inside, a blast of air was pumped through layers of charcoal and iron ore, intensifying the fire. Limestone in the furnace helped separate out the metal in the ore. Molten cast iron ran from the base of the blast furnace into a trench where it could run, cool, and solidify. This main trench led to several smaller trenches, which resembled a mother pig feeding her litter of piglets. As a result, cast iron produced in these troughs was called pig iron. The pig iron could be poured directly into molds or melted again to make objects such as cast-iron stoves, pots, pans, cannons, cannonballs, and bells.

skill of the metalworker making it. In the 200s BCE, metalworkers in India used crucibles to smelt wrought iron with charcoal to make high-quality wootz steel. In China, craftsmen also created high-quality steel.

STEEL WEAPONS AND TOOLS

Much of the early interest in steel was for its use in weapons and tools. Swords made from steel were tough, flexible, and easily sharpened. Soldiers realized steel could be an advantage on the battlefield. Armies from China, Greece, Persia, and Rome demanded steel for their weapons and armor. Some of the best-known bladed weapons in history, including Damascus swords and the katanas of Japanese samurai, were made from steel.

In addition to weaponry, steel was also used to make a variety of tools. Craftsmen created tools such as axes, chisels, and saws with steel tips to make them stronger and more durable. Yet steelmaking remained time-consuming and expensive. Through the 1700s, steel was produced in limited quantities by craftsmen who specialized in working with the metal. They produced handmade weapons, tools, and other products that were both beautiful and useful.

Damascus Swords

Made from steel, Damascus swords were well-known for their strength and quality. The swords were tough and shatter-resistant, and they could also be sharpened to a fine edge. Damascus swords could split a feather in midair and keep their sharp edges through many battles. They were made from wootz steel probably imported from craftsmen in Southern India or Central Asia. Damascus swords were easily recognized by wavy patterns on their surfaces that resembled flowing water.

Steel weapons and armor can now be seen in museums throughout the world.

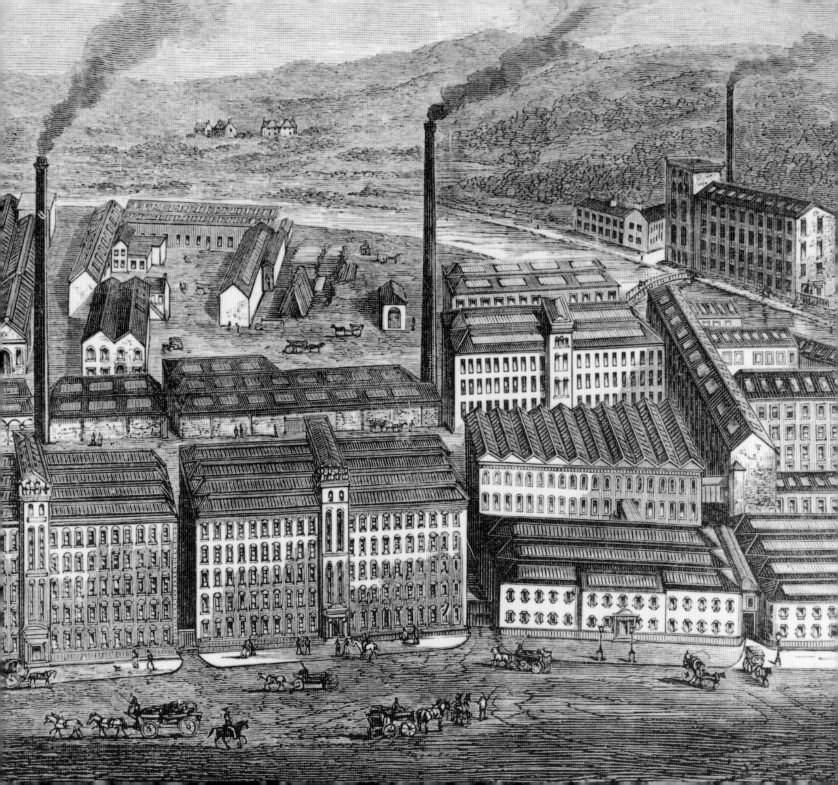

3 | STEEL AND THE INDUSTRIAL REVOLUTION

In the early 1700s, iron was the primary material used in industry. During the Industrial Revolution of the 1700s and 1800s, new inventions and innovations led to major changes in manufacturing and trade worldwide. By the end of the Industrial Revolution, steel overtook iron as the metal most used by the modern world.

COKE AND FURNACES

One important innovation for iron and steel production was the use of a coal product to fuel smelting furnaces. This change emerged because of a shortage of trees. In the 1600s, iron makers in Western Europe and Great Britain harvested forests for wood to fuel their furnaces. A single blast furnace consumed approximately 6,000 cords of wood each year, the equivalent of 240 acres (97 ha) of forest.[1] In Britain, deforestation became such a problem that the kings and queens issued royal edicts to ration woodlands. With the supply of wood limited, charcoal grew scarce and increasingly expensive.

The emergence of factories and other elements of industrialization brought steel to new prominence.

In the early 1700s, Abraham Darby, an Englishman who made cast-iron pots, searched for another fuel to smelt iron ore. He turned to cheap and plentiful coal. Previous attempts to smelt iron ore with coal had failed. Iron smelted with coal was too brittle to be used. Darby believed that roasting the coal to create a carbon-rich material called coke would remove the impurities in coal that made the smelted iron too brittle. In 1709, Darby successfully used coke in a blast furnace to produce pig iron. The use of coke allowed him to build larger furnaces, meaning he could smelt more iron. And because coke was cheaper than charcoal, he could smelt iron less expensively. Darby's innovation allowed him to make and sell his cast-iron pots at reduced prices.

HUNTSMAN'S CRUCIBLE STEEL

In the 1740s, Benjamin Huntsman, an English clockmaker, was unhappy with the quality of steel parts for his clocks. At the time, steelmakers typically made steel by layering wrought iron bars with

Industrial Revolution

Beginning in the 1700s and lasting through the early 1900s, many new ideas, inventions, and innovations dramatically affected the way people lived and worked. This period of great change is called the Industrial Revolution. During the Industrial Revolution, machines started doing the work of people. These machines could manufacture goods faster and cheaper than ever. Great

who lived far away. Inventions such as electricity and the telephone transformed daily life, bringing people closer together. Many people moved to cities, shifting away from agriculture and toward factory work. The Industrial Revolution began in Britain, but it soon spread to continental Europe and the United States. In many ways, the Industrial Revolution improved life for people

powdered charcoal and heating them for a long period of time. This increased the carbon content of the metal alloy. The process was very time-consuming, taking days or weeks to complete. In addition, the quality of the resulting steel was uneven and too inconsistent for Huntsman's clock springs.

To solve this problem, Huntsman attempted to make his own steel. Using a clay pot called a crucible, Huntsman added iron chunks and other ingredients. He sealed the crucible and placed it in a coke fire. The blazing fire melted the contents inside the crucible and allowed the right amount of carbon to spread evenly through the iron. It created a high-quality, uniform steel. When the crucible was removed from the fire, workers tipped it to pour its liquid contents into molds. Using a crucible, Huntsman could make steel in relatively large quantities. Although English steelmakers were reluctant at first to adopt Huntsman's crucible technique, they eventually started using it and produced some of Europe's finest steel.

Bigger and Better Furnaces

Several improvements to iron smelting led to bigger and better furnaces. Iron smelters built large furnaces, with some of them reaching as high as 20 to 30 feet (6 to 9 m). They used powerful bellows to blow air into the furnaces. At first, some bellows were powered by horses or water. Later, steam engines ran blowers that could deliver a blast of air strong enough to blow a person off his or her feet. Large furnaces with powerful bellows could produce two to three short tons (1.8–2.7 metric tons) of iron daily. At first, iron makers used cold air to fan the furnaces' fires. In the early 1800s, they discovered that if the air was heated before it was forced into the furnace, the furnace could smelt iron using much less fuel.

In the late 1700s, metalworkers used steel to make the hard, sharp edges of many tools and machines. Workers created steel drill bits, saws, and cutting edges for a variety of tools. As the Industrial Revolution continued, the demand for iron and steel increased.

HENRY CORT'S FURNACE

Henry Cort, an Englishman who supplied iron and steel to shipbuilders, designed a new type of furnace to improve the quality of pig iron. Cort's furnace had two chambers, one for the coal fuel and a second for cast-iron bars. The flame from the first chamber passed over the cast-iron bars in the second chamber. The iron melted. The melted cast iron settled into a puddle at the bottom of the second chamber. Carbon escaped the molten iron by mixing with oxygen in the air to form carbon dioxide. As the amount of carbon in the molten iron decreased, the iron's melting point rose, causing the puddled iron to stiffen. Using long rods, workers stirred the puddles in a process called puddling. They pulled a lump of malleable wrought iron from the chamber. Although the process was long, it was not as difficult as hammering the pig iron. And with a reduced carbon content, the pig iron was tougher and less brittle.

In 1783, Cort devised a way to run the hot, malleable iron through a series of grooved rollers, which turned it into bars without hammering. Using his rolling process, Cort could make wrought iron bars faster than anyone using a hammer. Cort's innovations opened the door for the mass production of iron and steel needed for the Industrial Revolution. Industrial-scale rolling mills emerged to create sheet iron and steel for a variety of uses.

Cort's puddling process made it possible to produce iron and steel in much higher volumes than ever before.

STEAM AND STEEL

With forest supplies dwindling, Europeans switched from wood to coal as a main source of fuel. Dug deep underground, coal mines often flooded. In 1712, British inventor Thomas Newcomen developed the first practical steam engine for pumping water from the mines. Powered by coal, his engine heated water until it produced steam that was powerful enough to turn a machine's gears and turbines. With Newcomen's steam engine to pump water from the mines, coal miners could dig deeper into the earth.

In 1765, Scottish inventor and instrument maker James Watt repaired a Newcomen steam engine. While doing so, he realized the engine was extremely inefficient. It lost too much steam as it worked. Watt made several changes to the steam engine, producing a version that generated more power from the same amount of coal.

The improved steam engines were rapidly put into use. They powered mills, factories, breweries, and other industrial facilities. Around 1776, English industrialist John Wilkinson added a Watt steam engine to a blast furnace. The steam engine increased iron production and lowered its cost. The demand for cheaper iron increased. In England, iron makers produced approximately 18,000 short tons (16,000 metric tons) of pig iron in 1740. By 1780, pig iron production more than doubled to 40,000 short tons (36,000 metric tons). By 1800, it soared to 160,000 short tons (145,000 metric tons). And by 1840, production skyrocketed to 1.7 million short tons (1.5 million metric tons), more than 10 times the amount produced only 40 years earlier.[2]

The Industrial Revolution had spread throughout Europe by this time. Enterprising innovators took the latest techniques and technologies overseas to North America, Japan, and the rest of the world. Economies that had relied on wood, stone, and brick now were based on iron and steel. Iron became an integral part of construction and transportation. Railroad companies built tracks

made from wrought iron rails. Great iron-hulled ships carried thousands of passengers. And iron buildings soared high into the sky.

STEEL AND AGRICULTURE

Although steel was not yet being mass-produced, it was having a significant impact on agriculture. In the 1800s, life on a farm was not easy. Farming tools were mostly simple, handheld, and made from iron. In North America, farmers turned land into farmable soil using plows to loosen up the soil and allow moisture to reach the roots of crops. Plows were often made of wood, with cast-iron parts added to the cutting edge. Yet the thick, sticky soil of the Midwest stuck to wood and iron plows. And the iron cutting edges often broke in the heavy soil.

In 1837, a young blacksmith named John Deere fitted a steel blade onto a plow. Steel was harder than iron and would not break as easily. In addition, the steel blade could be made very smooth so that it cut though the soil without sticking. Deere's steel plow worked much better to cut into thick soil. It allowed farmers to cut furrows into the soil faster. Word spread slowly about Deere's plow. By 1842, Deere sold 100 plows. By 1849, more than 2,000 plows had been ordered, and Deere set up a plow-making factory.[3] The steel plow became an essential tool of the American farmer.

4 | MASS PRODUCTION

Changing pig iron into the steel needed to make fine tools and machinery was very slow and expensive. As a result, through the early 1800s, steel remained a niche metal. It was used only in a limited amount of products. In the 1850s and 1860s, several new manufacturing techniques appeared that allowed steel to be produced faster and in greater quantities.

THE BESSEMER PROCESS

In 1854, Henry Bessemer, an English inventor, designed a new artillery shell that spun while flying for added stability in the air. When standard cast-iron cannons were not strong enough to shoot his new, heavy shell, Bessemer made a new cannon. He wanted to cast it from a stronger metal—steel. He quickly discovered the process for making steel was time-consuming and expensive.

Bessemer devised a new way to make steel. While working near a furnace, Bessemer noticed that if air was forced into molten pig iron under great heat, the iron could be changed into steel. He built a converter that used this idea. Approximately four feet (1.2 m) high, the converter had several pipes extending from its bottom that carried forced air

Technological advances in the 1800s revolutionized the steel industry, turning the metal into an important global commodity.

Before working on steel developments, Bessemer created improved typesetting machines and an efficient sugarcane-crushing device.

into the chamber. Bessemer poured molten pig iron into the converter and then blew air through the bottom of the converter through the pipes. For the first ten minutes, everything appeared to be working smoothly. Then, a large white flame burst from the converter's top, followed by sparks, explosions, and an eruption of liquid metal. Slag and hot metal flew into the air. The converter rocked with several explosions. Within another ten minutes, the eruptions stopped and the flame died down. The resulting molten metal, heated to higher temperatures than ever before, was a good quality steel that could be molded into ingots or bars.

Next, Bessemer adapted his new process so it could be used commercially. He experimented with several converter designs until he found the most efficient. By August 1856, he obtained a patent on his invention, which he called the Bessemer process. Bessemer's innovation revolutionized steelmaking. He created a cheap, fast way to make large amounts of steel. Whereas Huntsman's crucible steel method produced approximately 60 pounds (27 kg) of steel in two weeks, Bessemer's process produced 5 short tons (4.5 metric tons) of steel in 20 minutes. Bessemer began selling his steel at one-tenth of the price of his competitors.[1]

Iron makers came to Bessemer to see his new converter. They purchased licenses from him to use the new steelmaking process. Bessemer's steel was used to make tools, engines, steamboats, cannons, warships, bridges, buildings, and many other objects. Over the next 50 years, Bessemer's converter evolved into a 12-foot- (3.6 m) tall, black steel container that looked like an egg with an open top. It tilted to let workers pour in molten pig

William Kelly

Like Henry Bessemer, William Kelly of the United States also designed a converter to refine pig iron. The owner of an iron works, Kelly experimented with ways to save fuel costs in his furnace. He discovered a blast of air increased the temperature of the molten iron. He experimented with a series of furnaces to save fuel by this process. After several failures, Kelly succeeded in producing iron and steel with his process around 1850. He did not patent the process. Instead, he continued work in secret to improve the quality of the steel it produced. In 1856, Kelly learned Bessemer had obtained a patent on a similar process in England. Kelly objected to Bessemer's patent application in the United States. He showed his own experiments and was granted a US patent in 1857.

The Problem with Phosphorus

When British iron makers first attempted to use the Bessemer process, the steel they produced was very brittle. Immediately, they called Bessemer a fraud. In fact, Bessemer had been lucky. When he first made his steel, he had used pig iron that was very low in phosphorus, an element that makes steel brittle. When heated, phosphorus did not burn out of the molten iron, leaving the iron makers with breakable steel. Bessemer's steel was not brittle because he had used low-phosphorus ore from Sweden. However, low-phosphorus ore was scarce and expensive. A short time later, Bessemer and the British iron makers discovered adding limestone to the converter drew the phosphorus out of the pig iron. This discovery meant they could use iron ore to make strong steel even if it contained phosphorus.

iron. With the liquid pig iron inside and air blasting in, the converter became like a volcano. For ten minutes, a white flame rose toward the factory ceiling, sometimes reaching as high as 30 feet (9 m) as the carbon in the pig iron burned away.[2]

OPEN-HEARTH FURNACE

While Bessemer was perfecting his converter, German engineer Carl Wilhelm Siemens experimented with a new process, the open-hearth furnace. Originally developed for making glass, it was soon adapted to producing steel. During iron smelting, a lot of heat is lost in the air. Siemens figured out a way to capture this heat and use it to add more heat to the smelting furnace. He built a furnace with a shallow hearth that held molten metal and was exposed to flames above it. At each end of the furnace, a chamber captured heat from the hot exhaust gases and returned it to the furnace. The recycled heat increased the temperature of the incoming flame. This allowed the open-hearth furnace to reach very high temperatures. Under the high heat, the iron stayed liquid even after the carbon burned out. Steelmakers could add or subtract various ingredients to or from the liquid steel to make a high-quality steel. In 1864, Frenchman Pierre-Emile Martin further refined Siemens's process. He adjusted the location of the chambers. He also used scrap steel in the process, which reduced costs.

By 1900, the Siemens-Martin process passed the Bessemer process as the most efficient way to make steel. Although open-hearth furnaces were not as fast as Bessemer's converters, they allowed steelmakers to more precisely control temperatures and chemistry during smelting. This led to better quality steel. The open-hearth furnace could also produce larger batches of steel and could be used to recycle scrap metal.

MASS PRODUCTION

Within two short decades, innovations such as the Bessemer process and open-hearth furnaces

How the Bessemer Converter Worked

Bessemer's converter worked by using high-pressure air drafts to force the impurities out of molten pig iron. The converter was a large vessel supported on pivots. It had a single opening on the top. Solid pig iron was placed in the top and heated through the bottom. Once the pig iron melted, forced air was blown through and across the liquid metal. Instead of cooling the iron, the forced air reacted with impurities in the pig iron, including carbon, manganese, and silicon, and caused them to convert into a gas or a solid material called slag. This increased the temperature in the converter even more, causing more impurities to ignite. It also produced the violent sparks and flames that erupted from the converter's open top. Workers poured the molten steel from the converter into large molds, where it could be shaped for a variety of products.

One of Bessemer's first converters is now on display at the Science Museum in London, England.

changed the steel industry. Steel was no longer only made by artisans in limited quantities. Now it could be mass-produced in large quantities and at reasonable prices. In addition, the new processes allowed steelmakers to produce good quality steel in consistent shapes and sizes.

Now more readily available, steel became an integral part of many industries. Steel quickly replaced iron in the railroad industry. Early railroad tracks were made of wood, cast iron, or wrought iron. Although iron rails were an improvement over wood rails, they also had flaws. Iron rails were often unable to bear the weight of trains that were getting heavier, larger, and faster. Railroad companies found they needed to replace iron rails as often as every three months. No trains could run while workers made the replacements, which disrupted business. Officials of the Pennsylvania Railroad noted, "The rapid destruction of iron under the high speeds and heavy locomotives now used upon railways, has become a subject of serious consideration."[3] In the mid-1850s, the first steel rail was developed. It was put into a railroad trial in 1862. After two years, railroad officials said the steel rail significantly outlasted iron rails. As steel became more widely available and more reasonably priced, it quickly replaced iron in railroads. "Probably no other technological development has done so much to increase the capacity of the railroads and reduce their operating costs as this substitution of steel for iron rails," wrote the Pennsylvania Railroad's historians in its centennial history.[4]

Steel rails quickly spread across the country. The price of steel dropped from $140 a ton in 1872 to $35 a ton in 1882. At the same time, new production methods increased the availability of steel.

By the late 1800s, sturdy steel rails were carrying trains across the United States.

Between 1872 and 1882, American steel production jumped from 90,000 short tons (82,000 metric tons) to 1.5 million short tons (1.4 million metric tons). In 1880, 115,000 miles (185,000 km) of railroad track crossed the United States. Only 29 percent of this track was made with steel rails. By 1900, America had 258,000 miles (415,210 km) of track, and 93 percent of it was made with steel.[5]

With greater quantities of steel available, steel replaced iron in many construction projects. Steel framing and reinforced concrete led to the world's first skyscrapers. Built in Chicago, Illinois, in 1885, the ten-story Home Insurance Building was the first tall building supported by a steel skeleton of vertical columns and horizontal beams. The steel frame weighed only about one-third as much as a similar building made of stone would have.[6] In shipbuilding, steel replaced wrought iron plates. Steel was also used to make large turbines and generators, which enabled industrial factories to use the power of water and steam to operate machinery.

Barbed Wire Fences

Steel played an unexpected and important role in the American West. In the western United States, ranchers claimed land and raised livestock. Enforcing land claims, however, was difficult, and livestock often roamed outside a ranch's borders. Traditional methods to enclose land did not work well in the West. Fences of smooth wire did not hold livestock effectively. Hedges were difficult to grow and maintain. In the 1870s, barbed wire emerged as a solution. Barbed wire is a type of steel fencing wire with sharp points or barbs arranged at regular intervals along the wire. Barbed wire fences were the first wire fencing able to restrain cattle. They were also cheap and easy to set up and maintain.

5 | AMERICAN STEEL

In the United States, the Bessemer converter and the open-hearth furnace, along with the discovery of large deposits of iron ore, ushered in the age of steel and changed the country forever. In the mid-1800s, explorers traveling across the upper Midwest discovered large amounts of iron ore. Chemists analyzed the ore found near Lake Superior. They found it was free of phosphorus, which made it perfect for steelmaking. This discovery sparked a new rush to the region. Miners came from all over, including places as far away as Wales, England, Sweden, and Finland.

The American Civil War (1861–1865) brought the need for steel for railroads, telegraphs, steamships, and weapons. After the war ended, the demand for steel continued as construction across the country boomed. Railroads crossed the continent and opened up the western territories. Americans could travel and ship goods faster than ever before. Cities on the East Coast grew quickly, built with inexpensive steel girders and beams. Steel suspension bridges stretched across rivers and valleys. Passenger liners and navy ships discarded wooden hulls in favor of steel. Manufacturers discovered they could preserve food in steel cans. Farmers turned to steel too, buying steel machines and tools and using steel barbed wire to fence in their lands.

Enormous iron mines in northern Minnesota shipped their ore across the Great Lakes to steel plants in Ohio and Pennsylvania.

To meet the growing demand, new ironworks and steelworks sprung up in the United States. Iron and steel companies often built plants near rivers, which provided cooling water and transportation, and in areas where coal or iron ore were plentiful. Companies built mills in Pittsburgh's Monongahela Valley, on northeastern Pennsylvania's Lehigh and Conemaugh Rivers, and along the Mahoning and Cuyahoga Rivers in Youngstown and Cleveland, Ohio. Mills sprung up along the shores of the Great Lakes. They also emerged in areas where iron ore and coal were close to existing rail lines, such as Birmingham, Alabama.

Unskilled Workers

The adoption of Bessemer steel changed the type of worker needed in mills. While traditional iron mills typically employed skilled ironworkers, the new steel mills depended on machinery. With more of the process being mechanized, the plants no longer needed skilled master craftsman to run the mill. Instead, these machines could be operated by strong semi-skilled and unskilled laborers. While a skilled ironworker might take three years to learn his job, an unskilled laborer could learn how to operate machinery in only a few weeks. The increased reliance on unskilled workers allowed steel companies to take greater control of the mills. If workers protested conditions, they could be easily replaced with other unskilled laborers.

ANDREW CARNEGIE

One of the central figures in the growing steel industry was Andrew Carnegie of Pittsburgh, Pennsylvania. Born in Scotland in 1835, Carnegie immigrated to the United States with his family at age 13. The family settled into a slum section of Pittsburgh called Slabtown. From a young age, Carnegie was determined to take advantage of the opportunities around him. In 1853, he landed a job as the assistant to Thomas Scott, the superintendent of the Pennsylvania Railroad's western division. Taken under Scott's wing, Carnegie learned the railroad business.

In 1865, Carnegie left the railroad and formed the Keystone Bridge Company. He and his partners planned to build bridges with iron instead of wood, making them stronger and more durable. Over the next several years, he was involved in other successful business ventures, including the Freedom Iron Company.

On an 1872 trip to England to raise money for a bridge project, Carnegie visited a Bessemer steel plant. He realized the enormous commercial potential for steel. When he returned to Pittsburgh, Carnegie convinced his partners to construct the world's most modern and efficient Bessemer steel plant on the banks of the Monongahela River near Pittsburgh. He invested heavily in Bessemer converters, installing them at the new plant. He named the new plant after Edgar Thomson, the president of the Pennsylvania Railroad.

The opening of the Edgar Thomson Works in 1875 introduced cheap, plentiful steel to the region. Carnegie's timing was perfect. Iron rails used in railroads up to that time were likely to split and needed to be replaced frequently. In contrast, Bessemer steel rails lasted ten years. American railroad companies were ordering these rails from England. Carnegie planned to make them domestically in Pittsburgh. His first order was for steel rails for the Pennsylvania Railroad.

In his steel mills, Carnegie focused on efficiency. He hired engineers to streamline and mechanize the steelmaking process. His plants employed thousands of workers. Over the next 25 years, Carnegie's steel business became the world's largest. He was known for driving his managers and workers at a hard and dangerous pace. He was relentless at cost-cutting, always looking for ways to make steel more cheaply. He was also committed to adopting the latest technical innovations in his mills.

VERTICAL INTEGRATION AND ECONOMIES OF SCALE

Carnegie pioneered vertical integration, taking control over each part of the steel process. He consolidated several steel-related businesses, including steelmaking, ship and rail transport, and finishing plants. A large steel plant needed blast furnaces, foundries, rolling mills, and machine

Making Steel at the Edgar Thomson Works

In August 1875, Bessemer converters at the Edgar Thomson Works made their first batch of steel. Cold air was driven through the bottom of the furnace through the molten iron. The heat increased and burned out the impurities in the iron to form steel. Watching the process was incredible. It was described in an 1893 issue of *McClure's Magazine*:

> Out of each pot roared alternately a ferocious geyser of saffron and sapphire flame, streaked with deeper yellow. From it a light streamed—a light that flung violet shadows everywhere and made the gray outside rain a beautiful blue. A fountain of sparks arose, gorgeous as ten thousand rockets, and fell with a beautiful curve, like the petals of some enormous flower. Overhead the beams were glowing orange in a base of purple. The men were yellow where the light struck them, violet in shadow....
> The pot began to burn with a whiter flame. Its fluttering, humming roar silenced all else.[1]

shops to make plant equipment. Coke mines, iron fields, and railroads kept the mills supplied. Carnegie bought them all.

In 1881, Carnegie purchased a majority interest in the H. C. Frick Coke Company, which controlled the coal needed to make the coke used in his blast furnaces. In the deal, Carnegie also brought aboard Henry Clay Frick, a young self-made millionaire with a keen business sense. Carnegie now controlled all aspects of steel production, from ore to finished product.

In addition to expanding his business vertically, Carnegie understood the value of economies of scale in the steel industry. Economies of scale occur when the average cost of producing a product falls as the volume of output increases. This happens because the fixed costs of production are not directly related to the number of units made. In the case of steel, the large costs of building the plant and steelmaking machinery are fixed. As more steel is produced, these fixed costs can be spread out over more units. To increase the size of his company and take advantage of economies of scale, Carnegie purchased more steel mills. In 1883, Carnegie bought a plant from a rival steelmaker in Homestead, Pennsylvania. Then in 1890, he bought another mill in Duquesne, Pennsylvania, also along the Monongahela River. By the 1890s, the Carnegie Steel Company had become the world's largest and most profitable enterprise.

Carnegie made a fortune in steel. He was obsessed with technology and efficiency like no one else. His efforts to keep costs low and sell steel at lower prices than his competitors made his mills the most efficient in the world.

Steel made Carnegie one of the wealthiest people in human history

By the late 1890s, open-hearth furnaces had replaced the Bessemer process as the main method for making steel. Most of Carnegie's steel mills had changed over to open-hearth furnaces, as he believed they were the future of steelmaking. His Homestead plant was the world's largest open-hearth mill in 1890. Sixteen furnaces ran at a time. Each furnace produced 40 short tons (36 metric tons) of steel every six hours.[2]

Open-hearth furnaces were extremely hot, reaching nearly 3,000 degrees Fahrenheit (1,649°C). Working by the hearth was not an easy task. A worker who was responsible for adding carbon and manganese to the molten steel described the process in 1919:

You lift a large sack of coal to your shoulders, run towards the white hot steel in a hundred-ton ladle, must get close enough without burning your face off to hurl the sack, using every ounce of strength, into the ladle and run, as flames leap to roof and the heat blasts everything to the roof. Then you rush out to the ladle and madly shovel manganese into it, as hot a job as can be imagined.[3]

US STEEL

By 1900, steel had become a major global industry. The United States passed the United Kingdom as the world's largest steel producer. It was also the beginning of a great era of consolidation in the industry.

Steel for the Golden Gate Bridge was created on the East Coast and shipped through the Panama Canal to San Francisco, California.

BETHLEHEM STEEL

In 1903, Charles Schwab purchased a small steel company called Bethlehem Steel. Along with Bethlehem Steel president Eugene Grace, Schwab grew Bethlehem Steel into the second-largest American steel company, behind only US Steel. Bethlehem Steel focused its business on government contracts. During World War II (1939–1945), Bethlehem Steel was a large supplier of war materials.

Bethlehem Steel also produced construction beams for skyscrapers and bridges. The company's steel can be found in New York City's Chrysler Building. It also built San Francisco's Golden Gate Bridge.

After World War II, Bethlehem Steel doubled its capacity. Yet the company was slow to adopt new technologies developed in Europe and Asia. Bethlehem Steel went bankrupt in 2001.

In 1901, Carnegie sold his steel company to a group led by banker J. P. Morgan for $480 million, retired as the richest man in the world, and embarked upon a new career of philanthropy.[4] Morgan's group combined their interest in Carnegie Steel with the Federal Steel Company and other businesses to form the United States Steel Corporation. In its first full year of operation, US Steel made 67 percent of all the steel produced in the United States.[5] Elbert H. Gary became the corporation's first chairman.

Morgan had learned from Carnegie that integrating all of the steps of the manufacturing process into a single corporation could yield efficiencies in scale and processes. US Steel's original market capitalization was $1.4 billion dollars, which is approximately $40 billion in 2015 dollars.[6] It was the largest company in the world.

6 | LIFE OF A STEELWORKER

As the American steel industry experienced rapid growth in the late 1800s, many people flocked to mill towns in hopes of finding work. People who had grown up working on farms now took jobs as industrial steelworkers. Cheap labor poured in from overseas and from rural areas. A steady supply of workers allowed companies to keep wages low.

IMMIGRANT WORKERS

Immigrants from Europe arrived in the United States to work in the mills. In the 1850s, skilled workers from Germany, England, Ireland, or Wales typically immigrated to work in the American iron mills. These workers often arrived with entire families and quickly settled into permanent homes in mill towns, blending easily with existing Americans.

In the 1880s, immigrants from southern and eastern Europe arrived in the mill towns. Back in Europe, jobs were scarce and the men were desperate for work. The feudal estates where many peasants had worked in the past were breaking up, and the peasants were forced from the land with no prospects, money, or jobs. Most came alone, either as single men

Working in early modern steel mills could be hazardous.

looking for work or as married men with families back in Europe. Some of the first immigrant workers helped recruit others, writing letters about available jobs to people back home. Others helped new arrivals get settled.

Arriving in Steelton

In 1915, an immigrant ship carrying a load of Croatian workers arrived in Philadelphia. Even though the wages were low and the work was hard, the entire shipload was headed for Steelton, Pennsylvania, an industrial town outside Harrisburg. Upon arriving in the mill town, the new men followed friends or family through the mill gate and sometimes into the same mill department. At Steelton, Serbians and African Americans worked in the blast furnaces, while Croatians and Slovenians worked the open-hearth furnaces. Bulgarian workers ran the plant's railroad. Skilled workers were typically American, German, English, or Irish.

WORK IN THE MILL

Work in a steel mill was incredibly difficult. Workers entered as laborers, either in the mill itself or in the coke ovens, blast furnaces, or mill yard. They worked seven days a week, twelve hours a day. Workers in Carnegie's mills had a single holiday— the Fourth of July. The rest of the year, they worked. In the summertime, the heat of the mills was often unbearable. "Hard! I guess it's hard," said a laborer about his work at Carnegie's Homestead mill. "I lost forty pounds [18 kg] the first three months I came into this business. It sweats the life out of a man. I often drink two buckets of water during twelve hours; the sweat drips through my sleeves, and runs down my legs and fills my shoes."[1]

Workers often labored for hours without a break, with not even enough time to eat lunch.

Without an official break, some workers found ways to sneak a few minutes of downtime. "We stop only the time it takes to oil the engine," said William McQuade, a plate-mill worker in 1893, about a three- to five-minute break. "While they are oiling they eat, at least some of the boys, some of them; a great many of them in the mill do not carry anything to eat at all, because they haven't got time to eat."[2] In return for this effort, the average steel mill worker in 1890 earned approximately ten dollars a week.[3]

The long hours and backbreaking heavy labor of steel mills took their toll on workers. Many started work as teens, but few remained on the job into their forties. Yet despite the hard work, men took mill jobs because they paid well compared to other unskilled labor.

Besides being difficult, working in steel mills was dangerous. Workers only had two layers of wool long johns as protective gear. Gruesome injuries were common. "They wipe a man out here every little while," said a steel mill worker in 1893. "Sometimes a chain breaks, and a ladle tips over, and the iron explodes. . . . Sometimes the slag falls on the workmen. . . . Of course, if everything is working all smooth and a man watches out, why, all right! But you take it after they've been on duty twelve hours without sleep, and running like hell, everybody tired and loggy, and it's a different story."[4] Women and children living in the mill towns dreaded the sound of the factory whistle that signaled an accident had occurred.

MILL TOWNS

Mill owners often built company housing near the mills and rented it to workers. Many workers lived in these cramped and crowded towns because they could not afford to live further away and commute to the mills. Some single men lived in groups of three or four to a room.

People who lived in mill towns often had to deal with poor housing, smoky air, and polluted water. The mills spewed thick black smoke into the air that coated everything it touched with a layer of dirt. "The women in the steel towns fly a flag of defiance against the dirt," wrote journalist Mary Heaton Vorse about mill towns in Pittsburgh. "It is their white window curtains. You cannot go into any foul courtyard without finding white lace curtains stretched on frames to dry. Wherever you go, in Braddock or in Homestead or in filthy Rankin, you will find courageous women hopefully washing their white curtains. There is no woman

African-American Steelworkers

Before the American Civil War, thousands of African-American slaves were forced to work in the iron and steel industry in the Southern states. After the war, millions of former slaves entered the workforce. In the South, prejudice and racism remained, and African-American workers were shunned by Southern white trade unions. Large numbers of African Americans moved north to find work and a better life. Many found jobs in the steel mills of Pittsburgh, Chicago, and Maryland. In the late 1800s and early 1900s, the jobs given to African Americans were typically the dirtiest and most dangerous in the mill. Although the mills themselves were not segregated, African-American workers and their families often faced segregated housing and recreational facilities outside of the mill.

Towns built just for workers typically sprung up around steel mills.

so driven with work that she will not attempt this decency."[5]

Workers living in mill towns also dealt with polluted water. Mills dumped waste full of dangerous chemicals into nearby rivers. Fish died in the contaminated waters. Even the town's drinking water was contaminated from the chemicals.

7 | THE UNION ERA

During the Industrial Revolution, many people took mill jobs hoping for a better life. They quickly discovered mills were grim and dangerous places to work. Mill owners could treat workers this way because there were no regulations to protect employees. As long as there were people willing to work in the mills, mill owners had no incentive to change conditions.

If a worker complained about mill conditions, he could be blacklisted and labeled a troublemaker. Other employers in town would not hire someone who had been blacklisted. As a result, many workers did not speak out about mill conditions because they feared losing their jobs. Steel mills employed many thousands of semiskilled and unskilled workers. These workers had no effective voice to unite them.

EARLY STEEL UNIONS

In 1876, skilled iron puddlers and rolling mill workers joined together to form the first metalworkers' labor union, the Amalgamated Association of Iron, Steel, and Tin Workers. A labor union is a group of workers who bargain with company owners for better wages and safer

In the late 1800s and early 1900s, steelworkers unionized in an attempt to raise wages and improve working conditions.

Morewood Massacre

In 1891, conflict between the H. C. Frick Coke Company and mine workers escalated into violence. The miners, represented by the United Mine Workers of America (UMWA) union, demanded a pay increase and an eight-hour workday. Determined to break the union, Frick brought in strikebreakers and Pinkerton detectives. He evicted workers' families from company housing. On March 30, approximately 1,200 workers marched on Morewood, Pennsylvania, where the H. C. Frick Coke Company operated. They damaged the coke works. The Pennsylvania governor ordered the National Guard into Morewood. When approximately 1,000 strikers marched into Morewood on April 2, the armed guardsmen opened fire, killing seven workers.[1] Defeated, the striking workers returned to the coke factory by the end of May.

working conditions. If owners ignore the union's demands, the union can call a strike and workers will walk off the job. Sometimes during a strike, workers protest outside the company's buildings. Without employees working, mills cannot produce iron and steel and make money. As a result, a strike quickly gets the owners' attention.

Once formed, the Amalgamated Association focused its efforts primarily on improving conditions for skilled ironworkers. It had relatively little interest in improving working conditions and wages for unskilled and semiskilled steelworkers, even though they were the majority of employees in the mills. This prevented the Amalgamated Association from becoming an effective voice for workers in the steel industry.

OWNERS FIGHT BACK

Steel companies were not happy with the potential power of labor unions. They actively fought their workers' attempts to form a union. Most mill workers lived in mill towns run by the steel companies that employed them. The mill's owners hired the police and spied on workers. Workers attempting to organize a union were jailed, fined, or blacklisted.

Steel companies fired workers if they complained about long hours or working conditions. Some owners hired private detectives to spy on suspected union members and organizers. They fired union leaders and blacklisted them so they could not get a job at another mill. If a union called for a strike, some owners shut down the mill entirely. With the mill idle, the workers were not paid. In some cases, mill owners hired strikebreakers to cross picket lines and replace striking workers in the mill.

BATTLE OF HOMESTEAD

One of the most violent confrontations between a union and a steel company took place on July 6, 1892, at the Homestead Steel Works near Pittsburgh, Pennsylvania. A few years earlier, in 1889, Homestead's workers had gone on strike and won a three-year contract that provided good wages and better working conditions. But Homestead's owner, Andrew Carnegie, and his plant manager, Henry Clay Frick, were determined to lower the mill's production costs and regain control of the mill from the union.

With Carnegie's support, Frick cut wages and declared the mill nonunion. When the union refused to accept the new conditions, Frick announced he would no longer negotiate with it.

Carnegie and Frick believed the mill workers would disband the union in order to keep their jobs. Instead, the workers went on strike.

Frick locked out the striking mill workers. He built a fence around the Homestead plant and topped it with barbed wire and searchlights. Then Frick sent for 300 agents from the Pinkerton National Detective Agency to protect the mill's property. He planned to hire strikebreakers and reopen the mill without the striking union workers.

The heavily armed Pinkerton guards arrived by river barge in early July 1892. As the guards tried to land, thousands of striking mill workers and townspeople moved into position along the riverbank. The two sides fought, and shots were fired. The fierce battle lasted for 12 hours. In the end, the outnumbered Pinkertons surrendered. Seven strikers and three Pinkertons were killed.[2]

For several days after the battle, union workers controlled the town and the mill. On July 12, state militia arrived in Homestead. Some 8,000 heavily armed troops took command of the entire town.[3] The two sides settled into a waiting game. Eventually, the strike lost momentum and ended in November 1892. Local officials arrested strike leaders and charged them with murder. Carnegie banned the union from his mill, increased working hours, and lowered wages. The Homestead strike damaged the relationship between unions and management for decades.

GREAT STEEL STRIKE OF 1919

When World War I (1914–1918) broke out, employers wanted to ensure they could meet wartime production demands and did not want workers to strike. During this period, steelworkers negotiated increased wages and shorter workdays. As the war ended in November 1918, steelworkers expected the gains they had achieved during the war would continue.

However, as soon as the war was over, some anti-union employers attempted to roll back the workers' gains. They fired and blacklisted union organizers. They attempted to intimidate and spy on workers to prevent them from supporting union efforts. In Pittsburgh, steel companies pressured town leaders to ban union meetings. In western Pennsylvania, where several major steel mills operated, union opposition was intense. "There will be no meeting held in Duquesne," warned James Crawford, the town's mayor. "I'll tell you that Jesus

1901 Strike

After the formation of US Steel, the Amalgamated Association voted to require a steel company to sign a union contract for each of its plants. This demand became an issue in labor negotiations with US Steel. When no agreement could be reached, the Amalgamated Association called for a strike in 1901. US Steel argued it was not practical for the company to recognize unions in mills that did not already have them. When union leaders disagreed, US Steel began replacing strikers. The strike dragged on until September, when it was finally settled in favor of US Steel. The union's insistence on signing a union contract in all of a company's mills was not able to be enforced. The union emerged from the strike significantly weakened.

Christ can't hold a meeting in Duquesne."[4] Union organizers who tried to conduct a meeting were jailed and fined.

By the summer of 1919, unrest grew among mill workers. They felt betrayed by the broken promises of steel companies and the government to raise wages and improve working conditions. Workers demanded action. Finally, workers called for a strike on September 22, 1919, against US Steel. Workers at other steel companies also joined the strike. On that date, steel mills shut down across the United States. The strike eventually involved more than 350,000 workers and became known as the Great Steel Strike of 1919.[5]

Initially, the strike was a success as steel mills around the country shut down. Company owners fought back and portrayed striking workers as dangerous radicals who threatened the American way of life. Eventually, government officials called in the National Guard and federal troops to put down the strike in many cities. In some places, confrontations between troops and workers led to violence and some deaths. The striking steelworkers held out for three months. They eventually returned to the steel mills in defeat in January 1920. Although the strike involved thousands of workers at its peak, it did little to improve working conditions in the steel industry.

LABOR-FRIENDLY LEGISLATION

In the 1930s, changes in the federal government finally allowed steel unions to thrive. In 1933, Congress passed the National Industrial Recovery Act. Under this act, industry groups were to set minimum floors on prices, production, and wages to help the depressed economy. The act also guaranteed workers the right to organize and bargain collectively with management through representatives of their choosing. In 1935, the US Congress passed the National Labor Relations Act, also known as the Wagner Act. The act set up a National Labor Relations Board and required employers to bargain in good faith with union representatives. At the same time, the Congress of Industrial Organizations aggressively organized unskilled workers.

In 1933, Labor Secretary Frances Perkins visited Homestead, Pennsylvania, to assess working conditions and build community support for the new federal legislation. Perkins was to represent the steelworkers in the negotiations. When Perkins arrived, town officials refused to give her permission to speak with a group of steelworkers. Undeterred, she met with the workers at a local post office, where the steel company had no control because it was federal property. In August, after pressure from Perkins and President Franklin D. Roosevelt, Pennsylvania's steel leaders signed the steel code, which set up a basic eight-hour day and forty-hour workweek. The code also made a

FDR's New Deal

The New Deal was a series of programs passed in the United States between 1933 and 1938. They included laws passed by Congress and executive orders from President Franklin D. Roosevelt. Roosevelt believed the power of the federal government was needed to get the country out of the Great Depression, a severe economic downturn that began in 1929 and persisted through the 1930s. His administration passed banking reform laws, emergency relief programs, work relief programs, and agricultural programs. Later New Deal reforms included a union protection program. The New Deal helped improve the lives of people in the midst of the Great Depression. It also set a precedent for the federal government to get involved in the economic and social issues of the country.

Frances Perkins, front right, met with steelworker representatives again in 1934 in Washington, DC.

recent 15 percent pay increase permanent, and it allowed for the organization of the Steel Workers Organizing Committee.[6] Although not perfect, the code of 1933 was the first step in improving the lives, work, and wages of steelworkers.

STEEL WORKERS ORGANIZING COMMITTEE (SWOC)

With the momentum of the New Deal federal legislation, John Lewis, founder of the Congress of Industrial Organizations (CIO), came to an agreement with the Amalgamated Association of Iron,

Steel, and Tin Workers in 1936. The Amalgamated would join with the CIO and form a new union called the Steel Workers Organizing Committee (SWOC).

Led by Philip Murray, the SWOC quickly became a strong organization. Headquartered in Pittsburgh, Pennsylvania, the SWOC led rallies in local mill towns and issued a nationwide radio address. Its organizers spread out into mill towns. They made it easy for steelworkers to sign up for the union, waiving the initiation fee and deferring the monthly dues. Within six months, the SWOC had signed up 125,000 members.[7]

In 1937, John Lewis met with Myron Taylor, the chairman of US Steel. Over a period of several weeks, the two men met in secret. In March 1937, US Steel announced it was fully recognizing the SWOC as a bargaining agent for its members. It also agreed to a substantial wage hike, the establishment of an eight-hour day and forty-hour workweek, payment for overtime, and the adoption of a basic grievance procedure for workers. Although several smaller, independent steel companies refused to recognize the SWOC at first, they eventually did by the early 1940s.

In 1942, the SWOC became the United Steelworkers of America (USWA). By the end of World War II, the steelworkers' union was firmly established. By the mid-1950s, the USWA had more than 1 million members.[8] The union achieved bargaining power for mill workers throughout the steel industry. In the years after World War II, the USWA won many benefits for it members, including pensions, vacation days, holidays, and medical benefits. Because of these gains, many steelworkers enjoyed a middle-class lifestyle.

8 | COLLAPSE OF AN INDUSTRY

After World War II, US trade and industry expanded. The postwar population boomed, which sparked a rise in construction and growth in cities. Large quantities of steel were needed for girders and reinforced concrete in tall buildings and other construction projects. In the years after World War II, 85 percent of the nation's products contained steel.[1]

The 1950s and 1960s brought growing prosperity and new innovations to the American people. Steel became an integral part of many products. By the 1960s, millions of consumers purchased mass-produced appliances. Refrigerators, freezers, washing machines, and dryers made with steel appeared in homes across the country. Even beer cans were made with steel.

Also during this time, the automobile quickly became a necessity for American families. Steel was used in the manufacture of cars. It was a key part of the related oil and gas industry, too. Steel machinery, pipes, and other equipment delivered and processed the oil and gas

Stadiums, elevated highways, and skyscrapers rose from US cities in the postwar era, boosting the demand for steel.

Standardized steel shipping containers became synonymous with global trade in the mid-1900s.

that Americans needed to power their vehicles and appliances.

With manufacturing booming, companies needed a way to safely ship all of these products. Designed in 1955, the steel shipping container proved to be a strong, safe method of transporting goods. Steel shipping containers carried products by road, railway, and ship.

By 1955, American steelmakers produced 117 million short tons (106 million metric tons) of steel annually, almost one-third more than their largest output during World War II.[2] America's largest steel company, US Steel, was making as much steel as the United Kingdom, France, and the Soviet Union combined. Still, there were signs of trouble. American steelmakers continued using traditional steelmaking methods and technologies. They were not innovative. Meanwhile, steelmakers in Europe and Asia were making investments in new technologies.

Specialized steel applications, such as long-distance pipelines, may have requirements that must be met by steel designed with specific properties.

HIGH STRENGTH, LOW ALLOY STEELS

Worldwide, steelmakers experimented with ways to make stronger steel designed for specific uses. When they added controlled quantities of different elements to melted iron ore, they created new high strength, low alloy steels (HSLA). HSLA steels have a much greater strength-to-weight ratio than traditional carbon steel. In cars, HSLA steels allowed vehicles to be strong and safe, and at the same time lighter and more fuel-efficient.

HSLA steels can be customized to have specific qualities. For example, the oil and gas industry has special requirements for its steel needs. The industry constructs giant pipelines

across all types of terrain and conditions to transport oil and gas. Pipes stretch across giant deserts, through frozen tundra, and under the ocean. No matter the conditions, the steel pipes need to be tough, so no leaks or explosions occur. The pipes also need to be easily welded, so no cracks or leaks occur at the joints connecting different pipe sections. To meet these needs, the steel industry developed a special HSLA steel.

DUAL-PHASE STEELS

Creating another type of advanced steel involves changing the steel's phase, or the crystalline structure in which its atoms are arranged. Manufacturers can roll the steel, heat it, and rapidly cool it to carefully control this structure. They end up with steel containing two phases of crystals: ferrite and martensite. The amount of each phase in the steel causes the properties of the steel to vary. This type of steel is called a dual-phase steel.

Fine control over the steel's properties can give manufacturers the exact combination of strength and ductility they are looking for. For example, carmakers can produce steel that is strong enough to keep passengers safe while light enough to keep the car's weight down and reduce fuel costs. David K. Matlock, a professor at the Colorado School of Mines, says, "You get the final structure you want, and create the final properties you need for the specific design."[3]

NEW PROCESSES AND TECHNOLOGIES

While steelmakers experimented with HSLA steels, they also developed new processes and technologies to make steel faster and more efficiently. In addition, steelmakers improved how they cast and rolled steel to create sheets, shapes, and steel forms. While some of these improvements came from traditional steelmakers in the United States and Europe, others were developed by new steelmakers in Japan and Korea.

One new technique, basic oxygen steelmaking (BOS) was invented in the 1940s by Swiss steelmaker Robert Durrer and refined by an Austrian company. Similar to the Bessemer converter, BOS uses blowing oxygen to lower the carbon content of molten pig iron and change it into low-carbon steel. The BOS process is very fast. Modern basic oxygen furnaces (BOFs) can change iron into steel in less than 40 minutes, compared to 10 to 12 hours in an open-hearth furnace. They

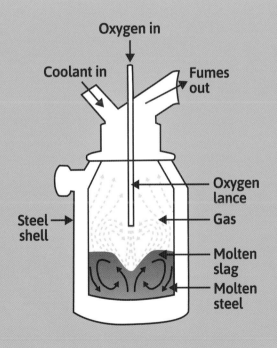

Basic Oxygen Furnace

In basic oxygen furnaces, pure oxygen rather than normal air is used. This results in higher-quality steel. Scrap metal is combined with molten iron at extremely high temperatures. Then, oxygen is blown into the mix at supersonic speeds for approximately 20 minutes. Molten steel collects on the bottom, and molten slag floats above it.

also use less energy. In addition, BOS increases the productivity of workers. Between 1920 and 2000, the labor needed in the steel industry decreased from more than 3 worker-hours per ton of steel to only 0.003.[4] Many manufacturers took advantage of the increased speed and lower energy use of BOS and replaced open-hearth furnaces with BOFs. Today, BOFs produce approximately 70 percent of the world's steel.[5]

In the 1960s, increasing amounts of scrap steel from vehicles, household appliances, and industrial waste became available. Scrap steel was plentiful and cheap. If steel manufacturers could figure out how to reuse it, they could reduce costs and help recycle waste. To use scrap steel, steelmakers turned to the electric arc furnace (EAF). EAFs had first been developed in the late 1800s and were mostly used to create specialty steel and alloys. EAFs use a high-power electric arc instead of a flame to melt scrap steel. Oxygen is blown into the furnace to drive out impurities. During the melting process, elements can be added to create the correct chemistry in the resulting steel.

EAFs were well-suited for recycling plentiful scrap steel. An EAF can be loaded with cold or preheated scrap steel or pig iron. Electrodes strike an arc and generate high temperatures to melt the scrap. The EAF process is fast, usually taking less than two hours to convert scrap steel into new steel. In addition, EAF furnaces are fairly inexpensive to build.

The increasing popularity of EAFs to recycle scrap steel in the 1960s opened the door for mini mills. In the United States, traditional integrated steel mills were common. Integrated mills were large and expensive to build. They consisted of large-scale plants that included both iron and steelmaking facilities. They often used open-hearth or BOFs. They required a blast furnace to provide the melted iron for the BOF. Some also included areas for turning steel into finished products. In contrast, a mini mill is a smaller-scale steelmaking plant. Using an EAF, a mini mill makes new steel from scrap. These mills are smaller and simpler to build and operate than traditional mills. Because they require a smaller initial investment, they opened the door for new companies to enter the industry.

Recycling Scrap

The scrap iron and steel used in electric arc furnaces comes from a variety of sources. Some scrap is generated during the steelmaking process. Other scrap comes from demolished buildings, old vehicles, and unused appliances and machinery. According to the World Steel Association, approximately 550 million short tons (500 million metric tons) of scrap are melted and used to make new steel each year.[6]

In addition to new methods for making steel, steelmakers came up with new ways to cast or pour molten steel. Traditionally, molten steel was poured into stationary molds to form large blocks called ingots. The ingots were rolled into steel sheets or into smaller shapes and sizes. A new technique called continuous casting poured molten steel continuously into a mold along a conveyor system, which created a long length of steel called a strand. The steel strand could be cut into slabs, which were much thinner than ingots and were easier to roll into sheets and other steel products.

OVERSEAS INNOVATIONS

By 1957, the American steel industry was still thriving. US companies made nearly half the world's steel and enjoyed healthy profits. Workers were also doing well. Unions had bargained for good wages, and hourly rates had steadily risen since the end of World War II. Steelworkers were solidly part of the American middle class, and they enjoyed health care and pensions.

After World War II, countries in Europe and Asia began to rebuild steel mills and factories damaged during the war. While rebuilding, they adopted many new steelmaking innovations. Europeans and the Japanese were quick to adopt BOFs to replace damaged and outdated equipment. In particular, Japan became an increasingly competitive steel producer. Borrowing from American and European expertise, the Japanese converted most of their steelmaking to the BOS process. They built large blast furnaces to create the maximum amount of pig iron from ores. And with low labor costs and government support, they were able to make and export large amounts of steel at a low price.

In comparison, the American steel companies were slow to adapt and change. They received relatively little support from the US government compared to that received by companies in other nations from their own governments. While Japan was building bigger and better blast furnaces, the Americans maintained the status quo. By the early 1970s, US Steel operated 67 blast furnaces with an average annual output of 465,000 short tons (422,000 metric tons) each. In comparison Japan's Nippon Steel operated 25 blast furnaces with an average annual output of 1.8 million short tons (1.6 million metric tons) each.[7] In addition, American companies were slow to adopt new processes such as BOF and continuous casting. US Steel did not build its first BOF until the early 1960s. By 1970, 33 percent of US steel output was made by the BOF process. In contrast, 95 percent of Japanese-made steel used BOFs.[8]

UNABLE TO COMPETE

Large and inefficient, American steel companies found it increasingly difficult to compete with European and Japanese steelmakers. The foreign steelmakers, who had adopted new innovations, were able to make steel at a much lower cost. The price of American steel was also increased by labor costs. By the 1960s, the labor gains that steelworkers and unions had won resulted in American steelworkers being paid significantly more than European and Japanese workers.

Embracing Change

In the United States, metallurgist Ken Iverson built steel company Nucor's first mini mill at Darlington, South Carolina, in June 1969. While many American steel companies were slow to adopt the new steel innovations, Iverson believed in the potential of mini mills. The mini mill was built to supply a nearby Nucor steel joist plant with cheap, raw steel. But Nucor's cheap steel attracted outside buyers. The mini mill quickly became a profitable steelmaker. While other US steelmakers were declining, Nucor experienced rapid and consistent growth. Today, Nucor is one of the largest American steel producers and one of the world's largest recyclers.

In 1971, the United States lost its position as the world's leading steelmaker. The Soviet Union produced 120 million short tons (109 million metric tons) of steel compared to the US total of 109 million short tons (99 million metric tons).[9] Cheap imported steel flooded the US market. Supply was beginning to exceed the worldwide demand for steel.

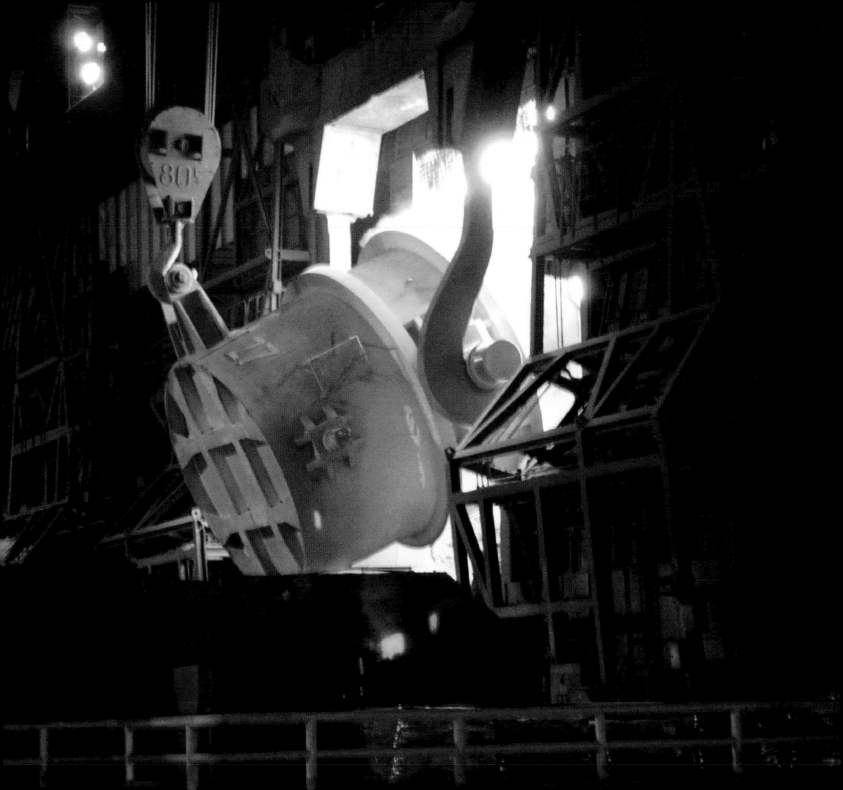

By the early 1980s, US steel companies were running at only 48 percent capacity, the lowest rate since the 1930s.[10] To cut costs, the companies laid off thousands of workers. Even so, the industry lost more than $3 billion in 1982.[11] The cost-cutting and layoffs continued in the 1980s. In 1983, US Steel shut down all or part of 28 plants, laying off 15,500 workers. The US Steel cutback hit cities such as Pittsburgh very hard. In the 1940s, US Steel operated 25 blast furnaces in Pittsburgh. By 1979, that figure had dropped to 13. By 1983, only two remained open.[12] The company closed mills up and down the Monongahela River Valley.

By 1987, the American steel industry capacity had fallen to 112 million short tons (102 million metric tons). As companies shut down and mills closed, more than half the country's steelworkers lost their jobs. Between 1975 and 1987, more than 265,000 jobs in the steel industry were lost.[13]

9 | REBUILDING THE MODERN STEEL INDUSTRY

By the 1970s, large integrated steel mills in the United States faced the challenges of outdated technology, too much capacity, and expensive labor and raw material costs. Competition from foreign steel companies and alternate materials such as aluminum and plastics also increased pressure on the steel industry. As the large steel mills struggled in the 1980s, new opportunities opened up for smaller companies willing to bet on new technologies.

EXPANSION OF MINI MILLS

At first, mini mills produced rebar, which are steel bars used for reinforcing concrete. Using scrap steel, mini mills could not initially produce the same quality of steel as large, integrated mills. Eventually, mini mill owners developed ways to produce higher quality steel that could be shaped and used in construction.

In 1987, steel company Nucor combined an EAF with compact strip production, a process that reduced the time and effort needed to produce thin steel sheets. The

The US steel industry had to make significant changes in the late 1900s to remain competitive.

innovation helped mini mills produce large quantities of sheet steel. Other new technologies allowed mini mills to use a wider variety of starting materials, instead of just scrap steel. The mills could now produce more types of steel, making them more attractive to operate. This improvement, combined with their lower cost to set up and operate, helped to drive the growth of mini mills around the world.

STEEL FOR EMERGING ECONOMIES

In recent decades, the global steel industry has shifted its focus from industrialized Western nations to emerging economies. Countries in the beginning stages of industrialization and development have enormous needs for steel to build cities and factories. Much of that steel production is done locally.

During this time, China has emerged as a leading steel producer. In the 1980s, China significantly expanded its steel production. Much of the increased production supported China's rapid development of cities and urban areas. Across the nation, cities and infrastructure were being built and modernized. To produce the steel needed for these projects, China built new steel plants. By 2011, the nation was the world's largest steel producer.

The American steel industry, devastated in the 1970s and 1980s, began rebuilding in the 2000s. Learning lessons from past mistakes, much of the rebuilding was based on new technologies. BOFs now make approximately 40 percent of American steel, with EAF responsible for the remaining 60 percent.[1]

The rapid growth of Chinese cities caused the country's steel needs to skyrocket.

HIGH-TECH STEEL

In recent years, modern steel mills have increasingly incorporated technology into the production process, resulting in improved quality, efficiency, and safety. In the United States, many modern mills use EAFs that produce iron and steel from scrap or iron ore. Many have finishing mills on site to convert the steel into products such as steel wire, pipe, bars, rods, and sheets. Finishing mills also coat some products to give the steel the characteristics required by a customer. Competition among steel mills has led many to specialize in certain types of steel production so that they can focus on a specific market. Some firms produce specialty alloys, adding materials such as nickel, chromium, manganese, or other elements to the steel. By varying the additions, companies can create thousands of steel alloys, each specially designed to have certain properties for a specific product.

In order to remain competitive in the global market, steel companies have turned to technology to improve production efficiency. They have invested in sophisticated technology to automate many parts of the steelmaking process. Some of the most physically demanding tasks were the first to be automated. Workers spend less time performing heavy labor. Instead, machines perform many of these tasks. Workers use computers to control these machines from air-conditioned rooms where they can watch the process through windows. Via computers, they monitor and move the iron and steel through the production process. Over the past 30 years, the automation of the steel production process has reduced the number of work-hours

China's Bird's Nest Stadium

In 2008, China hosted the Olympic Games. To prepare for the events, the country created the Beijing National Stadium. The 91,000-seat stadium was designed to incorporate elements of Chinese art and culture. The stadium's unique design looks like a jumble of exposed steel twigs. With its oval shape and twisted steel sides, it quickly became known as the Bird's Nest. The Bird's Nest is the world's largest steel structure. It is also one of the most complex stadiums ever built. To build the stadium, large tubes of steel were twisted around one another to create the nest-like shape. The stadium used 42,000 short tons (38,000 metric tons) of steel. It stretches 1,093 feet (333 m) by 965 feet (294 m). It soars 226 feet (69 m) tall.[2]

Modern steel mills are packed with computers and high-tech control systems.

required to produce a ton of steel by 90 percent.[3] The increasing use of technology in steel mills has opened the door for more high-tech jobs. For example, US Steel employees with PhD degrees study new materials under electron microscopes. "When you go into a modern steel mill, it's as high-tech as NASA," said Leo Gerard, the president of the United Steelworkers Union.[4]

Safety improvements in modern steel mills have also reduced the number of accidents. According to the World Steel Association, the injury rate for steelworkers around the world has dropped from 4.81 injuries per million hours worked in 2004 to 1.39 in 2014, an overall decrease of 71 percent.[5] In many mills, safety has become a top priority. Employees and management participate in training and on safety committees to develop procedures that keep workers safe. At the Gary Works in Indiana, employees from different departments are involved in the plant's safety committee, planning for safety and investigating accidents. Also, a joint team of union workers and management employees meets monthly to discuss safety issues and goals. Improvements in the protective gear worn by mill workers have also helped to reduce injuries and save lives. Flame-retardant suits worn in extreme-heat areas of the mill have reduced burn injuries, while hearing protection has reduced hearing loss and other related injuries. Workers wear safety glasses, face shields, and respirators to prevent the inhalation of dangerous gases.

The widespread collection and recycling of scrap steel has made the industry more sustainable.

THE FUTURE OF STEEL

For centuries, steel has played an important role in world history. Steel created the most prized weapons of the Middle Ages and built the machinery needed for the Industrial Revolution. Steel laid the foundation for transportation across vast distances, from railroads to ships to automobiles. It armored the tanks and warships that fought in two world wars. It also changed daily life, bringing about modern conveniences such as washing machines and refrigerators.

As important as steel has been to the advances and innovations of the past, steel is poised to have an equally important role in the world's future. The portion of people living in cities and urban areas is projected to grow worldwide from approximately 50 percent in 2010 to

approximately 70 percent in 2050.[6] To handle larger numbers of people, cities will need to expand and build. Constructing the necessary buildings and infrastructure will require steel.

Unfair Imports

The American steel industry faces a serious threat from foreign steel companies. Many of these steel companies are owned or subsidized by foreign governments. Some of these companies, particularly Chinese steel companies, have been accused of unfairly dumping steel into American markets. The practice of dumping occurs when a manufacturer exports a product to another country and prices it below the price charged in its home market or below its production cost. In response, the American steel industry has called on the US government to enforce trade policies that put all steel manufacturers on the same playing field. In May 2016, the US Department of Commerce announced it would impose heavy fees on steel from China and other nations to discourage dumping.

Steel will also play an important role in the energy industry. Steel pipes, machinery, and equipment will be needed as emerging countries exploit the conventional energy sources of oil, coal, and natural gas. And as the demand for renewable energy increases, steel will also be needed. Steel is used to build wind towers, solar and tidal power systems, and pipelines for water.

As the concerns over carbon dioxide emissions, the depletion of fossil fuels, and climate change increase, the steel industry is working to become more sustainable. Carbon dioxide emissions are a necessary part of the blast furnaces used to melt pig iron. However, the steel industry is spending billions of dollars annually to research new processes, products, and technologies to reduce carbon dioxide emissions in the steelmaking process. This research includes using different fuels and developing carbon capture technologies. Since 1990, the North American steel industry has reduced carbon dioxide emissions by 37 percent per ton of steel produced. It has also reduced the amount of energy needed to produce steel by 32 percent. As a result, the American steel industry uses less energy per ton of steel produced than any other major producer.[7] The United States is also a heavy recycler of steel.

As of 2014, the US steel industry had rebounded to operate more than 100 steelmaking facilities. According to Thomas Gibson, president and CEO of the American Iron and Steel Institute, steel remains a critical part of the American and world economy. "Many key markets and customer sectors rely on the success of the steel industry: automotive, construction, container, transportation and infrastructure, energy and national security—among others," he says. "We must continue to work together to ensure that making steel in America remains a fundamental pillar of our economy."[8]

Steel Utility Poles

In some communities, steel is being used to replace aging wood electric utility poles. Steel poles are easy to install, reliable, durable, and cost less over the pole's life cycle. In addition, using steel instead of wood has fewer negative effects on the habitats of threatened and endangered species. It also reduces the impact of hazardous emissions and wastes. Since 1998, nearly 1 million steel distribution poles have been installed across North America.[9]

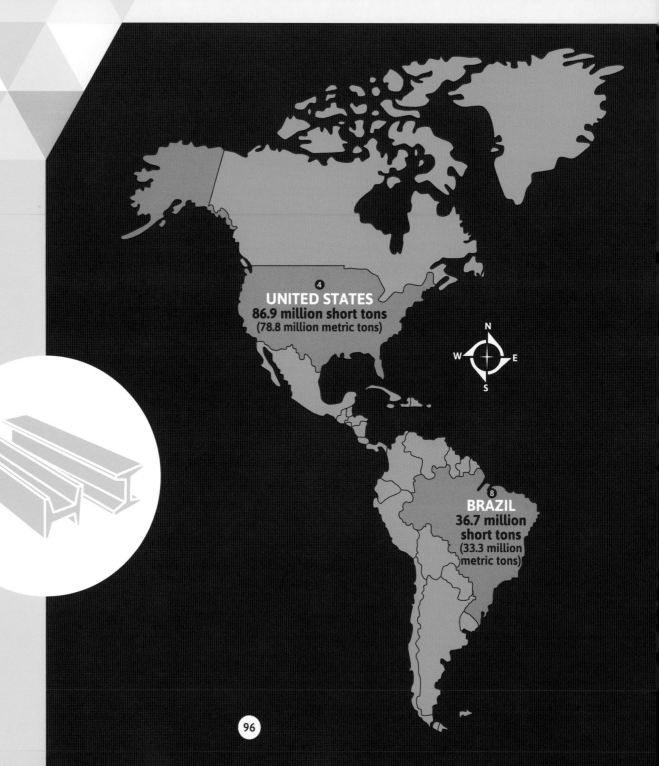

STEEL PRODUCTION 2015[10]

④ UNITED STATES
86.9 million short tons
(78.8 million metric tons)

⑧ BRAZIL
36.7 million short tons
(33.3 million metric tons)

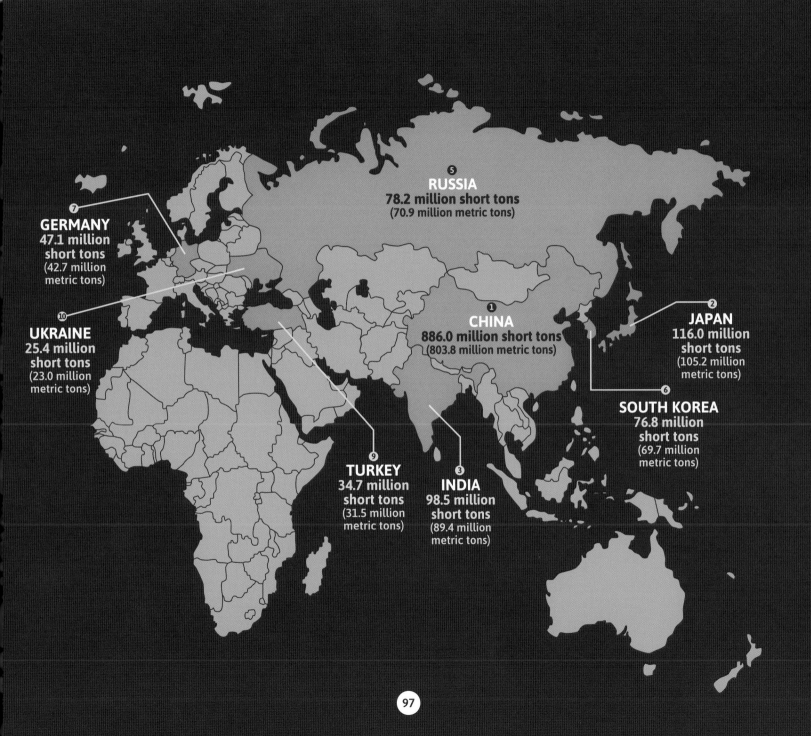

RUSSIA
78.2 million short tons
(70.9 million metric tons)

GERMANY
47.1 million
short tons
(42.7 million
metric tons)

UKRAINE
25.4 million
short tons
(23.0 million
metric tons)

CHINA
886.0 million short tons
(803.8 million metric tons)

JAPAN
116.0 million
short tons
(105.2 million
metric tons)

SOUTH KOREA
76.8 million
short tons
(69.7 million
metric tons)

TURKEY
34.7 million
short tons
(31.5 million
metric tons)

INDIA
98.5 million
short tons
(89.4 million
metric tons)

Timeline

1800 BCE
Early people discover that smelting iron ore produces a strong metal called iron.

1709 CE
Coke is first used to smelt iron ore, replacing wood and charcoal.

1740s
Benjamin Huntsman develops crucible steel.

1783
Henry Cort invents the steel roller for steel production.

1856
Henry Bessemer receives a patent for the Bessemer process, the first inexpensive industrial process for the mass-production of steel from molten pig iron.

1875
Andrew Carnegie opens the Edgar Thomson Works near Pittsburgh, Pennsylvania.

1876
The Amalgamated Association of Iron, Steel, and Tin Workers (AA) forms in the United States as a labor union of skilled iron- and steelworkers.

1892
The Homestead Steel Works strike turns deadly with several strikers and guards killed.

1901
US Steel is founded.

1903

Charles Schwab purchases Bethlehem Steel and eventually grows it into the second-largest steel company in the United States.

1914–1918

World War I increases the demand for steel weapons, vehicles, and other products for war.

1919

Steelworkers walk off the job in the Great Steel Strike of 1919, but eventually return to work without achieving significant gains.

1936

The Steel Workers Organizing Committee forms to negotiate for better wages and working conditions for steelworkers.

1939–1945

World War II results in heavy demand for steel for weapons, military equipment, railways, and ships.

1970s

American steel companies struggle with excess capacity, high costs, and increased competition from foreign steel producers.

1983

After a series of layoffs and closures, only two US Steel blast furnaces remain open in Pittsburgh, down from a peak of 25 in the 1940s.

2000s

The American steel industry rebuilds, using technologies such as BOFs and EAFs.

Essential Facts

IMPACT ON HISTORY

For more than a century, steel has been an integral part of the industrial world. Steel replaced iron in the railroad industry, allowing railroad companies to build tracks across countries and continents. Steel was essential to many construction projects, from bridges to buildings. In shipbuilding, steel replaced wrought iron plates. Steel was also used to make large turbines and generators, which allowed factories to use the power of water and steam to operate machinery. It also brought lifestyle goods such as refrigerators, freezers, washing machines, dryers, and automobiles to American families. Today, steel touches almost every part of modern life. People rely on steel for housing, transportation, energy production, tools, health care, and food and water supplies.

KEY FIGURES

▶ In 1856, Englishman Henry Bessemer invents the Bessemer process, a cheap, fast way to make large amounts of steel.

▶ In the late 1800s, Andrew Carnegie builds the Carnegie Steel Company into the world's largest and most profitable enterprise. He pioneers vertical integration, control over each part of the steel process.

▶ In 1876, the Amalgamated Association of Iron, Steel, and Tin Workers forms as the first union of steelworkers. However, it focuses its efforts on improving working conditions for skilled ironworkers and does little for unskilled steelworkers.

▶ In 1936, the Steel Workers Organizing Committee (SWOC) forms a union for skilled and unskilled steelworkers. In 1937, the SWOC negotiates increased wages and better conditions with US Steel. In 1942, the SWOC becomes the United Steelworkers of America (USWA).

▶ The American Iron and Steel Institute promotes the steel industry in the United States, working to influence public policy and educate the public.

KEY STATISTICS

▶ In its first full year of operation, US Steel made 67 percent of all the steel produced in the United States.

▶ Modern basic oxygen furnaces (BOFs) can change iron into steel in less than 40 minutes, compared to 10 to 12 hours in an open-hearth furnace.

▶ The steel industry directly employs approximately 142,000 people in the United States, and it directly or indirectly supports almost 1 million US jobs.

▶ By 2011, China was the world's largest steel producer, making more than 680 million short tons (617 million metric tons) of steel per year.

QUOTE

"We enjoy the benefits of steel in all aspects of our lives. From the moment we wake up until we go to sleep at night, we rely on steel in almost every aspect of our day."

—Thomas Gibson, president and CEO of the American Iron and Steel Institute

Glossary

alloy

A material made by combining two or more metals or a metal and another material.

bellows

A device with an air bag and two handles, used to blow air into a fire.

Bessemer process

A process for making steel that blows air into molten pig iron through the bottom of a converter.

blast furnace

A furnace used to produce iron from iron ore.

cast

To form an object by using a mold.

coating

A protective layer applied to the outside of a material.

corrosion

The breaking down of a material, especially a metal, through chemical reactions.

crucible

A small cylinder-like container made of fired clay used to produce high-quality crucible steel.

ductility

The ability to be hammered into thin wires without breaking.

ingot

A block of metal formed into a particular shape for further processing.

integrated mill

A large-scale plant that combines iron smelting and steelmaking facilities and may also include facilities for turning steel into finished products.

Additional Resources

SELECTED BIBLIOGRAPHY

Misa, Thomas J. *A Nation of Steel: The Making of Modern America 1865–1925*. Baltimore, MD: Johns Hopkins UP, 1995. Print.

Stoddard, Brooke. *Steel: From Mine to Mill, the Metal That Made America*. Minneapolis, MN: Zenith Press, 2015. Print.

"The White Book of Steel." World Steel Association. World Steel Association, 2012. Web. 13 Aug. 2016.

FURTHER READINGS

Carmichael, L. E. *Amazing Feats of Civil Engineering*. Minneapolis, MN: Abdo, 2015. Print.

Gillam, Scott. *Andrew Carnegie: Industrial Giant and Philanthropist*. Minneapolis, MN: Abdo, 2009. Print.

WEBSITES

To learn more about Big Business, visit **booklinks.abdopublishing.com**. These links are routinely monitored and updated to provide the most current information available.

FOR MORE INFORMATION

For more information on this subject, contact or visit the following organizations:

American Iron and Steel Institute

25 Massachusetts Avenue Northwest, Suite 800
Washington, DC 20001
202-452-7100
http://www.steel.org

The American Iron and Steel Institute is an association of North American steel producers. It works to influence public policy, educate the public, and support a steel industry that manufactures products that meet society's needs.

Steel Manufacturers Association

1150 Connecticut Avenue Northwest, Suite 1125
Washington, DC 20036
202-296-1515
http://www.steelnet.org

The Steel Manufacturers Association consists of 28 North American steel producers, who account for more than 75 percent of domestic steelmaking capacity. The association advocates for its members in public policy, provides a forum to exchange technical and operational information, and serves as a source of information about the steel industry.

Source Notes

CHAPTER 1. STEEL: A CRITICAL INDUSTRY

1. Leah Burrows. "Super-Slick Material Makes Steel Better, Stronger, Cleaner." *Harvard University*. Harvard University, 20 Oct. 2015. Web. 11 Aug. 2016.

2. Chris Woodford. "Iron and Steel." *Explain That Stuff*. Explain That Stuff, n.d. Web. 12 Aug. 2016.

3. "Profile 2016." *American Iron and Steel Institute*. American Iron and Steel Institute, 2016. Web. 12 Aug. 2016.

4. "Goal: Steel, Our Most Sustainable Material." *SteelWorks*. American Iron and Steel Institute, 2016. Web. 12 Aug. 2016.

5. "The White Book of Steel." *World Steel Association*. World Steel Association, 2012. Web. 12 Aug. 2106.

6. "World Steel in Figures 2016." *World Steel Association*. World Steel Association, 2016. Web. 12 Aug 2016.

7. Kelsey Mays. "The 2015 American-Made Index." *Cars.com*. Cars.com, 28 June 2015. Web. 12 Aug. 2016.

8. "Automotive." *World Steel Association*. World Steel Association, n.d. Web. 12 Aug. 2016.

CHAPTER 2. EARLY DAYS OF STEEL

1. Brooke Stoddard. *Steel: From Mine to Mill, the Metal That Made America*. Minneapolis, MN: Zenith, 2015. Kindle eBook. Location 137 of 4814.

2. Joseph Spoerl. "A Brief History of Iron and Steel Production." *Saint Anselm College*. Saint Anselm College, n.d. Web. 18 Aug. 2016.

CHAPTER 3. STEEL AND THE INDUSTRIAL REVOLUTION

1. Brooke Stoddard. *Steel: From Mine to Mill, the Metal That Made America*. Minneapolis, MN: Zenith, 2015. Kindle eBook. Location 137 of 4814.

2. Ibid. 520.

3. Michael Abrams. "John Deere." *American Society of Mechanical Engineers*. ASME, Apr. 2012. Web. 19 Aug. 2016.

CHAPTER 4. MASS PRODUCTION

1. Brooke Stoddard. *Steel: From Mine to Mill, the Metal That Made America*. Minneapolis, MN: Zenith, 2015. Kindle eBook. Location 646 of 4814.

2. Ibid. 657.

3. "First Steel Rails History Marker." *ExplorePAHistory.com*. Explore PA History, 2011. Web. 19 Aug. 2016.

4. Ibid.

5. Ibid.

6. "Home Insurance Building." *Wonders of the World: Databank*. PBS, 2001. Web. 19 Aug. 2016.

CHAPTER 5. AMERICAN STEEL

1. "The Steel Business: A Ferocious Geyser." *American Experience*. PBS, 2009. Web. 19 Aug. 2016.

2. "The Steel Business: The Open-Hearth Furnace." *American Experience*. PBS, 2009. Web. 19 Aug. 2016.

3. Ibid.

4. "Rags to Riches Timeline." *American Experience*. PBS, 2009. Web. 19 Aug. 2016.

5. "About Us." *US Steel*. US Steel, 2015. Web. 19 Aug. 2016.

6. Brooke Stoddard. *Steel: From Mine to Mill, the Metal That Made America*. Minneapolis, MN: Zenith, 2015. Kindle eBook. Location 926 of 4814.

Source Notes Continued

CHAPTER 6. LIFE OF A STEELWORKER

1. "The Steel Business: The Lot of a Steel Worker." *American Experience*. PBS, 2009. Web. 19 Aug. 2016.

2. Ibid.

3. Ibid.

4. "The Steel Business." *American Experience*. PBS, 2009. Web. 19 Aug. 2016.

5. "Steel City and Mill Towns." *ExplorePAHistory.com*. Explore PA History, 2011. Web. 19 Aug. 2016.

CHAPTER 7. THE UNION ERA

1. "Morewood Massacre Historical Marker." *ExplorePAHistory.com*. Explore PA History, 2011. Web. 19 Aug. 2016.

2. "Homestead Strike Historical Marker." *ExplorePAHistory.com*. Explore PA History, 2011. Web. 19 Aug. 2016.

3. Ibid.

4. "The Great Steel Strike of 1919 Historical Marker." *ExplorePAHistory.com*. Explore PA History, 2011. Web. 19 Aug. 2016.

5. "Postwar Labor Tensions." *Digital History*. Digital History, 2016. Web. 19 Aug. 2016.

6. "Frances Perkins Historical Marker." *ExplorePAHistory.com*. Explore PA History, 2011. Web. 19 Aug. 2016.

7. "United Steelworkers of America Historical Marker." *ExplorePAHistory.com*. Explore PA History, 2011. Web. 19 Aug. 2016.

8. Michael S. Mayer. *The Eisenhower Years*. New York: Infobase, 2010. Print. 494.

CHAPTER 8. COLLAPSE OF AN INDUSTRY

1. Brooke Stoddard. *Steel: From Mine to Mill, the Metal That Made America*. Minneapolis, MN: Zenith, 2015. Kindle eBook. Location 1359 of 4814.

2. Ibid. 1370.

3. Henry Fountain. "Many Facts, and Phases, of Steel in Cars." *New York Times*. New York Times, 14 Sept. 2009. Web. 19 Aug. 2016.

4. "Basic Oxygen Furnace." *International Iron Metallics Association*. International Iron Metallics Association, 2016. Web. 19 Aug. 2016.

5. "How Is Steel Produced?" *World Coal Association*. World Coal Association, 2016. Web. 19 Aug. 2016.

6. "Raw Materials." *World Steel Association*. World Steel Association, n.d. Web. 19 Aug. 2016.

7. Brooke Stoddard. *Steel: From Mine to Mill, the Metal That Made America*. Minneapolis, MN: Zenith, 2015. Kindle eBook. Location 3547 of 4814.

8. Ibid.

9. Ibid. 3641.

10. Ibid. 3749.

11. Ibid. 3549.

12. Ibid. 3833.

13. Ibid. 3844.

CHAPTER 9. REBUILDING THE MODERN STEEL INDUSTRY

1. "How Steel Is Made." *SteelWorks*. American Iron and Steel Institute, 2016. Web. 19 Aug. 2016.

2. "Beijing's National Stadium." *Design Build Network*. Kable, 2016. Web. 19 Aug. 2016.

3. "Steel Manufacturing Industry." *College Grad*. College Grad, 2016. Web. 19 Aug. 2016.

4. David J. Lynch. "Pittsburgh's Heart of Steel Still Beats Amid Transformed City." *ABC News*. ABC News, n.d. Web. 19 Aug. 2016.

5. "Safety and Health." *World Steel Association*. World Steel Association, Apr. 2016. Web. 19 Aug. 2016.

6. "The White Book of Steel." *World Steel Association*. World Steel Association, 2012. Web. 12 Aug. 2106.

7. "Steel Industry Reductions in CO2 Directly Tied to Energy Intensity Reductions." *SteelWorks*. American Iron and Steel Institute, 2016. Web. 19 Aug. 2016.

8. "Profile 2016." *American Iron and Steel Institute*. American Iron and Steel Institute, 2016. Web. 12 Aug. 2016.

9. Ibid.

10. "Top 10 Steel Producing Countries in the World." *WorldAtlas*. WorldAtlas, 2016. Web. 1 Sept. 2016.

Index

ABOUT THE AUTHOR

Carla Mooney is the author of several books for young readers. She loves learning about people, places, and events in history. A graduate of the University of Pennsylvania, she lives in Pittsburgh, Pennsylvania, with her husband and three children.